# The Encouraging Mentor

**Your Guide to 40 Conversations that Matter**

A how-to manual for mentors, teachers, coaches, and those who care.

Brian Raison, PhD

WESTBOW
PRESS®
A DIVISION OF THOMAS NELSON
& ZONDERVAN

Copyright © 2024 Brian Raison, PhD.

All rights reserved. No part of this book may be used or reproduced by any means, graphic, electronic, or mechanical, including photocopying, recording, taping or by any information storage retrieval system without the written permission of the author except in the case of brief quotations embodied in critical articles and reviews.

This book is a work of non-fiction. Unless otherwise noted, the author and the publisher make no explicit guarantees as to the accuracy of the information contained in this book and in some cases, names of people and places have been altered to protect their privacy.

WestBow Press books may be ordered through booksellers or by contacting:

WestBow Press
A Division of Thomas Nelson & Zondervan
1663 Liberty Drive
Bloomington, IN 47403
www.westbowpress.com
844-714-3454

Because of the dynamic nature of the Internet, any web addresses or links contained in this book may have changed since publication and may no longer be valid. The views expressed in this work are solely those of the author and do not necessarily reflect the views of the publisher, and the publisher hereby disclaims any responsibility for them.

Any people depicted in stock imagery provided by Getty Images are models, and such images are being used for illustrative purposes only.
Certain stock imagery © Getty Images.

Cover photograph by Tracy L. Csavina.

ISBN: 979-8-3850-0989-3 (sc)
ISBN: 979-8-3850-0990-9 (hc)
ISBN: 979-8-3850-0991-6 (e)

Library of Congress Control Number: 2023919275

Print information available on the last page.

WestBow Press rev. date: 01/24/2024

# Early Praise & Reviews

*I have used these conversation starters with both industry and university audiences. I have found them particularly engaging and powerful.*
   - Nathan Whitaker, #1 NYT Bestselling Author (with coach Tony Dungy), Super Bowl champion, and international speaker.


*"Cor," the Latin root of en-cour-age, means – heart. I've seen how Brian Raison's life, and his book, winsomely come alongside and mentor human hearts into flourishing lives. Mentored adults often shape cultures, nations, and a world awaiting hope. I urge you to meet Brian in the pages of this great book, and in person. For the joy.*
   - Kelly Monroe Kullberg, Author, *Finding God at Harvard*; Co-author, *A Faith & Culture Devotional: Daily Readings in Art, Science & Life*; Founder, the Veritas Forum


*In a noisy world we can all benefit from more conversations that matter. This book shows you how to start these conversations to be a more effective mentor and leader.*
   - Mark Sanborn, international bestselling author of eight books including *The Potential Principle* and *The Fred Factor* (which has sold 1.6 million copies).

*Questions are the real currency. These 40 conversations will help you and those you mentor literally talk your way right into tomorrow. It's the toolkit for mentoring made easy—but with all the robustness and depth of a good mentoring relationship.*

    - Chad Littlefield, Bestselling author of *Ask Powerful Questions: Create Conversations that Matter* and Founder of weand.me

*Great mentors are actually artists. They see possibilities in persons that have yet to be seen. Mentors help students become who they really are. Most students do not understand who they are, and even more imagine who they can become. Brian Raison has been mentoring people for 30 years. His book embodies that long and rich experience. I recommend this book to anyone who desires to help others become who they are really meant to be.*

    - James L. Heft, SM, PhD - Scholar in Residence, University of Dayton; Founder and President Emeritus, Institute for Advanced Catholic Studies (IACS) at USC

*This book gives the reader a toolbox, and it provides the necessary delicate balance between personal care and professional management.*

    - Christine D. Townsend, PhD, Professor Emeritus, Texas A&M University

*Brian's work offers accessible and proven methods for making human connections in your mentoring role. He offers real world examples of fostering deep and human relationships that can encourage individuals and collectively transform the world.*

    - John Noltner, Founder and Executive Director, A Peace of My Mind - https://apomm.net/

# Contents

Preface ................................................................................... ix

SECTION 1: Introduction ...................................................... 1
- Your Personal Connection to Mentoring ........................... 3
- Encourage and Challenge ................................................. 5
- Answers Are Cheap. Questions Are the Currency. ............ 6
- Formal, Informal, Nonformal ........................................... 7
- Unimaginable Potential .................................................... 9
- Naming Potential in Your Mentee .................................... 9

SECTION 2: Your Approach ................................................ 13
- Using this Resource ........................................................ 15
- Using this Resource with Groups ................................... 15
- On Teaching ................................................................... 18
- Start at the End. ............................................................. 19
- Start with Humility. ....................................................... 20
- Start with Yourself. ........................................................ 21

SECTION 3: The 40 Conversations ..................................... 23

This section contains the 40 conversation-starting prompts with background information that will help you launch a meaningful talk.

**Initiating Growth:**

1. The Mentoring Launch Conversation ......................... 25
2. The Being Remembered Conversation ....................... 30

3. 5 Things to Have, Do, Help, and Be: A Personal Futuring Exercise ................................................................. 31
4. The Bucket List ..................................................................... 33
5. The Values Review ................................................................ 36
6. Your Personal Mission .......................................................... 38
7. Leveraging Gratitude ............................................................ 41
8. Building Curiosity ................................................................ 44

**Deepening Connections:**

9. From Why? to What? ........................................................... 46
10. Helping Your Mentees Feel Safe ......................................... 52
11. What's Your Biggest Fear? A Check-in for Mental Health ....... 55
12. Bravery. Failure. Kindness. .................................................. 58
13. Joy vs. Happiness: Finding Fulfillment in Work and Life ....... 62
14. Remembering to Listen (to Others and Yourself) ................ 65

**Advancing the Career:**

15. Who You Are vs. What You Do .......................................... 71
16. What's Motivating Your Mentee? ........................................ 73
17. Change. Growth Mindset. Ambiguity. 3 Skills for Career Advancement ............................................................. 76
18. Reframing 6 Stages of a Career (from Ladder to Scaffold) ...... 79
19. Handling Critics and Criticism: A Growth Mindset Approach .. 82
20. Providing Clarity ................................................................. 86
21. Triangulating Your Skills, Abilities, and Interests to Find Your Future .................................................................. 88
22. The Resume & Cover Letter (Helping your mentee achieve their next position) ................................................... 89
23. Real Interview Tips that Work ............................................ 92
24. The Stay Interview: Is Staying an Opportunity? .................. 94
25. Financial Health: 2 Keys for Success Today and in Retirement (Live and Give) .................................................. 96

**Expanding Points of View:**

26. E+R=O (Event + Response = Outcome) ................................. 103
27. Circle of Control: Shift Your Focus; Reduce Worry .............. 106
28. Hidden Diversity: A Mentoring Conversation ...................... 109
29. Seek Diverse Relationships ...................................................... 112
30. Building Your Emotional Intelligence (EQ) ......................... 115
31. Building Your Social Intelligence ............................................ 117
32. Generation C: Mentoring for Connectivity ........................... 119
33. Spirituality & Faith Traditions ................................................ 122
34. Changing Perspective: Embracing the Art of Possibility ........ 126

**Anytime Conversation Prompts:**

35. Perspective Shifting ................................................................ 129
36. The Charles Schulz Mentoring Challenge: Embracing Contentment ............................................................................ 131
37. Building Trust ......................................................................... 134
38. The Power of Vision: An Indispensable Skill ........................ 136
39. Storytelling: A Useful Tool in Any Career ............................ 139
40. Leading with Humility ............................................................ 141

- 20 Bonus Questions to Use Anytime ...................................... 146

**SECTION 4: Teaching & Engagement Strategies** ........................ 149

This section outlines why teaching is foundational to mentoring relationships and provides basic, research-based approaches that anyone can use without additional training.

1. Reach Before You Teach Connection Strategies for Mentors, Teachers, Coaches, Supervisors, and even Families. .... 152
2. Connection Before Content .................................................... 157
3. Recognizing Potential .............................................................. 158
4. Creating Serendipity; Believing in Your Mentee ................... 160
5. Pedagogy vs. Andragogy ........................................................... 163
6. Transfer of Knowledge ............................................................. 165

7. Recognizing 8 Smarts ............................................................ 166
8. 12 Considerations for Engagement (Teaching Approaches for Mentoring) .................................................. 168
9. Write Your Teaching / Mentoring Philosophy Statement ....... 176

SECTION 5: The Summary .......................................................... 179

Acknowledgements ....................................................................... 182

About the Author .......................................................................... 183

**Also Available:** *40 Conversations: A Guided Journal for Personal and Professional Growth.* This is a companion workbook for mentees featuring questions from "The Encouraging Mentor." ...................................................................... 184

# Preface

In late August 2023, I had just finished teaching my first class of the new semester. It was an undergraduate course on personal and professional development offered to second year students (or sophomores as we used to call them) here at The Ohio State University where I serve as a professor. As soon as the last student left the classroom, I had just enough time to dash across the street and join a small group of fellow faculty, friends, and one retiree for lunch.

At some point, our conversation drifted to career paths. My brain was on high alert because these were things I wanted to share with my undergraduates, especially in their second year as some were still determining majors or perhaps discovering new fields or directions they might take in their studies and future careers.

As the conversation ensued and people told their stories, I was fascinated by one theme I had not anticipated. Repeatedly, I heard individuals mention *luck*, or *chance* as having a major role in their careers and lives. Three who mentioned this were professors. They each acknowledged times in their life when they *"luckily took an assignment"* or were *"in the right place at the right time."* They said those moments had made all the difference in their career and subsequent success.

The last person to share was a 91-year-old retiree, Henry Brecher, from the OSU Byrd Polar Research Center. His story was the most captivating. As a child, he had escaped the Nazi expansion in Austria, his homeland. His parents sent him away to stay with family in Croatia, but those caring parents were not able get out. Henry subsequently had to move twice more as the Nazis expanded their reach into Yugoslavia and Italy. He eventually made it to the United States through a displaced persons program and was able to stay after the war. Here, he attended high school, and his grades were good. He was able to go to college and became a mechanical engineer. But after a year or so in his first job, he began looking for something more exciting.

> *"Engine testing was a little boring. I wanted some adventure. One of my friends saw a small ad on a bulletin board looking for people to go to Antarctica. Neither of us met the qualifications, but we applied anyway and were both chosen. What luck! So many times in my life. . . I've been so very lucky."*

His early life story in itself was astounding. And his career path was too. Perhaps more so was that he acknowledged time after time being lucky at critical points where his path turned. At one point, he even said maybe it was not so much luck, but *a higher power who directed the course of events.* Others in the group agreed, noting that there is so much we cannot understand or explain in our natural world.

As I continued listening, my brain was flooded with memories of very specific times in my life when I was lucky enough to have a new door open, or a different door close. My siblings say I have astonishing luck. Perhaps looming largest was the fact that I was sitting at that table that day. You see, I had never planned to do more than go to college and get a degree so I could afford a nice car. That was the entirety of my life plan at the age of eighteen. Period. I had no vision beyond that. But over the years, I was extraordinarily lucky, blessed, had chance-encounters, or *was at the right place at the right time.* Doors opened. After obtaining a bachelor's degree and working ten years, I went back to school for a master's (and was lucky to have my tuition paid by my employer). Another six years passed, and I was in school to pursue the PhD (and again at no cost to me). But still, I had no vision of becoming a professor. That stuff was for other people. I still saw myself as a kid from southern Ohio. We generally don't do things like that. Or at least that was the story in my head.

However, along the way, doors opened, and opportunities arose. I had mentors (and family and friends and teachers and pastors and priests) who took the time to encourage me, challenge me, and help me recognize what I did not yet recognize in myself. Now I was teaching in the classroom, and at this particular lunch table, a fellow professor sharing *my* story of luck.

Luck is the intersection of preparation and opportunity. This is my favorite definition. But it begs the question: Can we create it? I believe there is a way to make luck happen.

This book shares forty conversations that matter. I've designed tools that will help both you and those you mentor create your own luck. The forty conversations are the *preparations*. Those are the first (and necessary) components. The intersecting arcs of *opportunity* come every day. They're around every corner. They spring from both good and bad events. We only need watch for them and recognize when there's a new possibility. Mentorship and encouragement will help that recognition to occur.

My challenge to you is to use these tools to help others create their own luck. Or at least to help them with *preparation* so that they recognize it when they arrive at an *intersection*. Then if random chance, karma, luck, or a higher power helps with the intervention or opportunity, all the better. This book is filled with encouraging challenges that will help those of you who mentor (and even you, the reader) be prepared.

Section 1

# Introduction

## Your Personal Connection to Mentoring:

Think about a time when someone encouraged you.

Please pause for a moment and sincerely give this a try. Picture that person in your mind. You may or may not remember their exact words, but I am nearly certain you remember how you felt when they shared a bit of their time to help you in some way. To me, this is one of the best feelings ever. Anytime we are encouraged, our brain chemistry kicks into gear. The dopamine neurotransmitters get to work. We feel motivated and productive. If we pay attention, we might even notice a sense of gratitude and generosity emerging in the afterglow.

Where does this all come from? Without doing a deep dive into emotional and social intelligence (Goleman, 1995 and 2006, respectively), most of us can anecdotally understand that encouragement produces results. Whether you are recalling a time of encouragement at an early age or later in life, the positive feedback more likely than not spoke to you. It helped.

Before proceeding, I must pause for a moment to address readers who may be having difficulty recalling times of encouragement. There are many who did not have family or friends who spoke positive messages into their lives. Some readers have received seemingly unending streams of negative feedback. *"You never do anything right." "Your opinion doesn't matter."* Research shows that even a few messages like that can literally block out the positive moments of encouragement that have occurred from time to time. If you are one who has had those negative experiences (or if you are working with someone in that category), you might be surprised to learn that mentoring others can help counteract some of that negativity and fill in some of your personal needs in this realm. Practicing encouragement is a curious thing. It helps us heal.

When we invest time in mentoring and encouraging others, two very different things happen. First, we send a positive outright message that attempts to help another person. Simultaneously, when we deliver that message, we gain an internal boost in *our* brain chemistry that simply feels good. The new research on this change in brain chemistry is fascinating. It confirms what wisdom writers and effective leaders have known for centuries: *putting others first improves our personal lives and helps make our world a better place.* This is a remarkable truth.

So, regardless of your predominate life experience (in being encouraged or not), pause again and dive deeper into a moment when you did receive encouragement. What was the situation? Had you accomplished something? Had you failed at something? What words were used? Dig down. Try to remember the emotions you felt when someone spoke a positive message to you.

For me, I can remember my great aunt Ima and uncle Bob speaking words of encouragement into my life as clearly as if it happened only yesterday. This was their habit of conversing. They were natural encouragers, and perhaps without knowing the extent, they changed my life for the better.

>
> **Here's our story:**
>
> Aunt Ima and Uncle Bob were two of the folks I admired most in the world. They often visited us at my grandparents' house where we lived in a small town along the Ohio River for many years after my folks' divorce. The thing I remember so clearly is they always commented on my work. "Why… what a good boy Brian is," my aunt would say in her thick West Virginia accent. "He's just so helpful."
>
> Little did they know I was just cleaning up and doing dishes so my grandmother would not fuss at me. But Mamaw didn't really mean anything when she fussed. It was mostly an act. It was her way of encouraging us, while simultaneously saying, "I love you, and I want you to become a responsible adult someday."
>
> It took me years to realize everything that was happening during these times together. Slowly, I have realized that

while I gained a lifetime of encouragement from my aunt and uncle, they were getting encouragement from me as well. In watching me laugh and play and enjoy some extra special activities my family could not afford (like taking me to the Cedar Point amusement park on Lake Erie), I now understand that they needed someone, a twelve-year-old boy, to bless. You see, they had lost their son (who was about my age) to leukemia just a year or so earlier. And they wanted to share that love they had for him in every positive way they could.

What a blessing, for me and others they encountered. They're now gone physically from this earth, but they live on every single day in me and in others they loved and encouraged.

I formally wrote down my life mission nearly twenty years ago. On that piece of paper, I wrote that I am going to be an encourager to others. Anyone I meet. Anywhere. Any day. My prayer is that I will honor my aunt Ima and uncle Bob all my days and pass their love on. In short, if you can tap into a strong motivation for encouraging others, your mentoring will become exponentially influential.

## Encourage and Challenge

*How can you tell if someone needs encouragement?* The easy answer is simply check for a pulse. Whether successful or struggling, we all need encouragement.

But we also need to be challenged. These two seemingly disparate approaches can work together to help people flourish, develop their natural gifts and talents, and subsequently make their lives and our world a better place.

There are a myriad of definitions and nuances in mentoring. In ancient Greece, Homer defined a mentor as a wise and trusted counselor, a guide, or a teacher. I often think of a mentor as someone who has served in a similar role who can help another person acquire the necessary behaviors, knowledge, and attitudes to succeed. In this way, mentoring is closely related to coaching, but with an important difference. Coaches often direct action. They tell *how* to improve your form or clear the high bar. Coaches often help their charge stay accountable to defined goals or intentions as well. Effective mentors, on the other hand, use *questions* to *guide* their protégé and *influence* their thinking. They do not tell them *what to do* or *how* to do it.

## Answers Are Cheap. Questions Are the Currency.

Above, I noted that effective mentors use questions as their approach to guide and influence, as opposed to a coach who may use information (providing data or answers) to help someone improve. In today's increasingly automated world, generative AI (artificial intelligence) large language models provide unlimited answers to any question we ask. They do this with no human agency or ethical/rhetorical intelligence. AI can (and often does) hallucinate, returning false information and data that replicate the biases of what it is scanning. It is improving; but inherent challenges persist as computer scientists admit they do not know exactly what is happening in the AI black box.

Would you, for example, want to trust a non-human giving advice based on questionable (biased) data sources? I personally prefer facts that have been vetted or justified based on empirical data or lived experiences. AI cannot deliver that. AI simply provides generated information that can quickly become noise, a distraction from what really matters. This presents a grand challenge: *having too much data*. We become quickly overwhelmed with options.

There is an alternative approach to sifting massive amounts of data (generated answers). In our mentoring context, we are working to help someone find answers or directions that are genuine and meaningfully derived. One of the best ways to do that is to *ask them* a great question.

My absolute favorite connection and engagement guru is Chad Littlefield of http://weand.me. He works with organizations around the globe, helping them strengthen true connections so they can improve processes and strategies that move groups toward mission attainment. His techniques work equally well in mentoring. Chad summarizes this AI and information overload phenomenon succinctly. He says answers (data/information) are cheap. *Questions are the real currency.*

Questions can help us, our mentees, or groups *"talk our way into the future."* Chad outlines an approach in which we use questions to help us clarify what we want and then prompt us to begin taking steps to get there.

So what if we quit trying to find answers, and begin crafting better questions? Might this help those individuals and groups we lead or mentor find better answers? Chad and I believe so.

In my nearly forty years of professional experience working in private industry, local government, non-profit management, and higher education (not to mention firefighting, the building trades, volunteer management, retail sales, and the gig economy), I have discovered good mentoring conversations can *simultaneously* challenge *and* encourage people when done at the right time and in the right manner.

Finding great questions is key, not just spewing information. Whether your mentees are co-workers, colleagues, students, those you supervise, or even family members, mentoring can be a powerful tool anyone can deploy. But how you approach mentoring is critical. Determining the right questions matters. Your *approach* determines your effectiveness.

## Formal, Informal, Nonformal:

Many of us have experienced mentoring programs that are fancy, formalized, and sometimes forced. Even if they have good question prompts or outlines, many are less than stellar. Some formal programs have even driven people apart. In response, a number of organizations shifted to embracing *informal* approaches; but these often result in people simply having coffee or lunch, and only minimal progress or advancement, if any, in personal or professional development is realized. Informal mentoring rarely works.

There is an alternative.

I began using a *nonformal* mentoring approach patterned on constructs of nonformal education theory. Here, mentors are equipped with tools they may deploy as needed based on the situation or goal and based on the mentee's current need. This allows for flexibility in timing, a critical component of personal growth. In short, hearing or learning something at the right time—when they are ready for it—makes all the difference in whether someone grows exponentially or simply keeps treading water. Nonformal mentoring can help you create those moments.

You need not become a mentor (formally, informally, or nonformally) to encourage someone and/or challenge them to grow. Anyone can use a question-based approach to help. All it takes is a small investment of your time.

*The Encouraging Mentor* offers mostly one-page outlines that provide you with deeply engaging formative questions to launch conversations that matter. The tools can be used by anyone without any formal training. I designed them as simple conversation starters that can be used whether you have five or fifty-five minutes to chat. Many of the tools can also be used with both small and large groups to foster introductions, interactions, and to reenergize groups mid-meeting. (Read more about this in Section 2.)

The nonformal approach guides you to use prompts found in this book to have brief conversations at that right time. This can help someone achieve their best self in their career or life. More importantly, *this encouragement might also simply help someone make it through the day.* Encouragement can reenergize. It can help people flourish. Encouragement shines light in darkness. Encouragement, one needed word at the right time, can literally save a life.

## Unimaginable Potential:

The conversation starters in this book aim at one thing: to tap into the unimaginable potential that exists within every single person on earth. I have it. You have it too. Everyone does. Mark Sanborn, author of *The Potential Principle*, says even those who are the best in the world have additional potential. We simply need to pause, reflect, find (or rediscover), and employ it. Few can summon it on their own. Most of us need an outside view or nudge to unearth or reach the *unimaginable* level. It's there, but we must follow a process or a path to reach it.

My goal is that each mentoring module or activity in this book will offer insight, while providing a specific action you can take today to encourage or mentor someone. The modules are designed to be cumulative. As a result, this is a process that takes time. While moving through the process, think of each activity or conversation as an *experiment*. This concept also comes from Chad Littlefield (http://weand.me) who suggests that every icebreaker or activity is actually an experiment. He claims that if we embrace it as such there is no harm in a failure, but great potential for gain when it works.

So are you ready to give mentoring a try? Are you ready to experiment? Are you ready to help someone discover their unimaginable potential?

If so, allow me to pose an overarching challenge that underscores the ultimate job of a mentor. I challenge you to *observe* your mentee, identify one or two aspects of their potential, and then call it out. This may sound simplistic or superfluous, but *naming* is powerful.

## Naming Potential in Your Mentee:

*Observation* might be the most important thing a mentor can do. Here are two questions to ask yourself when you begin a mentoring relationship:

> *What do you see in your mentee that has not been made manifest to the rest of the world... yet? What spark do they possess that needs fanning to become a flame?*

Observing and naming that spark can encourage someone you are mentoring onward to a path that can change their life for the better. Those changes will subsequently ripple out to their family, friends, coworkers, and networks. Your observation and encouragement could literally start a sequence of events that can change the world for the better. There are numerous examples throughout history. Do not discount your potential to ignite this light.

Now, this might sound like an impossible (or at best, tricky) task. That is, what if you call out the wrong thing? Don't worry. There is one critical thing to remember. It is certainly possible that you observe and/or interpret the "wrong" thing. You might see something that is not their top or best attribute, and then encourage them to pursue it. Well, guess what? If they are encouraged to pursue *any* attribute that is positive in nature, they will grow personally and professionally. That is our aim in mentoring. In addition, whatever you see is likely seen by others. As your mentee advances in whatever you have named, other strengths will also emerge. Conversely, if you don't speak, they may never hear that positive observation from anyone else. May I say that again?

*If you don't speak, they may never hear that positive observation from anyone else.*

Here's how my mentor's positive observation looked for me:

> *In early 2008, I found myself at a crossroads and unable to decide how to proceed in my professional career. I'd made a habit of changing jobs (or at least the type of work I was doing in my job) every few years. I loved my work as an educator with OSU Extension (running our county 4-H program and doing community development work), but I felt like there was something more. I could not put my finger on it, but I knew I needed a change.*
>
> *At that time, our Extension Area Leader, Dr. Stephen Wright, was also serving (nonformally) as my mentor. Today, I can clearly remember our conversation (including the room*

*and table where we were sitting). He looked directly at me and said, "Brian. You have the ability within you. Just put the letters behind your name and any door can be opened."*

*At forty-four years of age, I still saw myself as a kid from Southern Ohio who worked hard, volunteered in the summers, and loved my family. I never imagined I could earn a PhD, become a tenured faculty member, and direct my trajectory… until that moment.*

As a mentor, you have the power to influence someone's life in one moment with just one comment, *naming* what you see in them that the world has not yet seen. Are you ready to give that a try? Remember, you need not have any experience. These 40 conversations will guide you step by step.

## For Additional Reading:

Goleman, Daniel (1995). Emotional intelligence. Bantam Books, Inc.

Goleman, Daniel (2006). Social Intelligence: The New Science of Human Relationships.

Littlefield, Chad (2023). We Connect. Online at: http://weand.me

Sanborn, Mark (2017). The Potential Principle. Nelson Books. Nashville, TN

# Section 2
# Your Approach

## Using this Resource:

I have compiled this collection of conversation starters in a workbook style that allows mentors (or supervisors, co-workers, coaches, parents, friends, etc.) to meet a mentee where they are. There is power in asking that right question and engaging in that *right conversation at that right time.* This logically necessitates investing time in getting to know your mentee first, even if you *think* you know them already. Conversation #1 provides two key questions to begin that process. I suggest starting there.

In general, I have organized the chapters (or conversation starters) to be used sequentially, beginning with discovery topics before moving deeper. As you get to know your mentee, you may identify a specific need that is pressing or that is hindering your conversation. In this case, feel free to scan the table of contents to find a relevant conversation pertaining to their need, and engage out of sequence. There is no problem in mixing and matching. The overall idea is to simply engage and encourage.

If you have been assigned someone to mentor or coach, you may already be acquainted with them at some level. In other cases, particularly within larger organizations, you may have never met. Regardless of your situation, each conversation holds the potential for discovery for your mentee, *and* for you, the mentor.

As noted, this collection is designed to allow you to begin mentoring with no formal training. It provides everything you need to start meaningful conversations, make connections, and encourage another person to move toward the potential that they have not yet recognized.

## Using this Resource with Groups:

As noted, many of the tools in this book can be used in group process facilitation and interaction. I have used the full *experiments* and extracted individual questions to launch meetings, particularly when there might be a difficult agenda that day. I have used a number of these conversations to start the very first day of class in the semester. This builds relationships and trust with my students. By asking an engaging question and prompting even brief interaction among meeting participants, the energy in the room rises.

Now, I'm just curious. Does it sound like I'm describing an icebreaker?

Please, strike that word from your vocabulary.

When I am invited by a college dean or department chair to facilitate a strategic alignment or planning session with their entire faculty (and when it may have been suggested that it was a mandatory four to six-hour meeting), the last thing attendees want to hear is, *"We'll be starting with an icebreaker."* Whether you are working with busy Tier 1 research university faculty or a just-as-busy local nonprofit volunteer board, all groups benefit by making a human connection prior to initiating deep brain work.

Just as you warm up your car engine for better performance and to produce heat to defrost your windshield on a winter day, warming up the brains of individuals in your group will produce better thinking, ideas, and connections to help move you toward your meeting objectives and/or organizational mission.

When using these with groups, I often skip the requisite pleasantries and immediately pose a question. This approach alone is an attention-getter. A quick, engaging discussion can powerfully awaken brains and ready them for your meeting.

I have also used many of these tools to reenergize a group mid-meeting. Just look around the table or room. Are eyes glazed over? Have most folks quit contributing? Are you, as the chair or meeting leader, feeling drained as you realize you're only halfway through the agenda? You would be amazed at what happens when you press pause on the agenda, have everyone stand, and engage in a connection experiment. My favorite reawakening tool (that I did not include as a full mentoring conversation) is below. It works great with individuals too. I have used it successfully hundreds of times. I learned it from my OSU colleague, Steve Brady, nearly twenty years ago.

### *Fold Your Hands*

Have everyone stand as they are able. Instruct them to fold their hands, interlocking their fingers. Ask, *"Which Thumb is on Top?"* (Some will find their right, others their left.)

Instruct them to *unfold* their hands and do it again, *this time with their other thumb on top.* Acknowledge, *"It feels a bit weird, doesn't it?"*

Now, have them fold their arms in front of their chest. They have done this a million times. It's natural. Ask, *"Which arm is on top?"*

Finally, ask them to try folding their arms *the other way* with the "wrong" arm on top. They may have to focus to find success. For most people, this is very awkward.

Debrief the experiment:

> "We are creatures of habit. Our brains are conditioned for our personal reality. So how can we (or our team) get out of our comfort zone and discover a different way of thinking, a new approach that might move us more quickly toward our goal? Like crossing our arms the "wrong" way, it might be uncomfortable at first. But let's challenge ourselves to be open to new, more diverse ideas and ways of thinking."

In addition to engaging or reenergizing, some of these questions can help your group members make connections they have never considered about their work, backgrounds, family, interests, faith, or lives. These reawakening tools will strengthen your team and simultaneously build your organizational culture. Even brief conversations such as these will build trust.

Okay. Have you guessed my secret yet? Yes, I am talking about using these conversation questions as *icebreakers*! They will work because they create human connection before diving into the requisite content. But please remember, never, ever use the term *icebreaker*.

Feel free to extract any question from the 40 conversation starters to use as an opener. Along with the *Fold Your Hands* experiment, two of my other favorites are the *Bucket List* and *Being Remembered*. Simply shift the questions: *"What's on our team / organization bucket list?"* And *"How do we want our team / organization to be remembered?"* They both awaken brains to think about perspective, possibility, and potential. I hope you'll give these and others a try.

## On Teaching:

Mentoring is a form of teaching. As noted above, I want you to understand some of the teaching practice that is happening as you engage. This will enhance your effectiveness as a mentor. Even some brief introductory knowledge on teaching can help significantly.

Think about a teacher or professor you may have had who possessed great expertise and real-world experience in a subject, but they did not know how to convey that information well, i.e., they were not skilled in teaching or instructing. This is quite common. Studies show that even a basic introductory seminar or outline on *how to improve your teaching* can help greatly. Among my faculty colleagues, we joke that the highest rated class of the semester occurs when we have a guest speaker from the *real world*. Students want authenticity. They want to situate learning in real life. Mentoring is no different.

In 2020, just as the covid pandemic occurred, the Michael V. Drake Institute for Teaching and Learning at The Ohio State University invited me to join the inaugural class of faculty fellows tasked with improving teaching engagement across the university. I had been experimenting with online strategies for engagement that seemed to resonate with my students, both at the undergraduate and the graduate level, as well as in my statewide outreach though the Cooperative Extension Service. I began formalizing (writing down) what I was doing. I subsequently began teaching seminars for our faculty and instructional staff on *engagement strategies* (for both online and in-person instruction) at Ohio State and soon, by invitation, at numerous other universities and professional association conferences around the country and internationally. These nonformal engagement strategies were resonating because they worked.

I continued honing my practice, and invested more time in reading, researching, and compiling ideas to improve engagement. I have included briefs on many of these strategies as well as ideas I personally adapted or developed in the Section 4 of this book. These teaching strategies and the conversation-starters are all grounded in andragogy (adult learning theory). I did this to assure the highest quality possible and to ensure meaningful dialogue would result as you pursue mentoring goals.

## Start at the End.

Since mentoring is a form of teaching, the "Teaching Engagement Background and Strategies" (Section 4) may be a good place to start your journey. Here, you will find several outlines, teaching approaches, thinking, and background information about teaching that will be helpful. These are very brief overviews that will set the stage for delivering the conversation questions and content found in this book. This section includes brief descriptions of things such as the transfer of knowledge and learning, Bloom's Taxonomy, Fink's Significant Learning, and other teaching practices. This background on how learning works may be instructive as you begin mentoring.

Please note, this is not required reading, but it will be helpful. Please also note that you need not worry about gaining a full understanding of pedagogical practice (not at all!). But as an educator, I am compelled to include this background. I often explain to my students *what* I'm doing as I teach so they will better understand the process, why it matters, and how future applications can be made. I call it teaching transparently. It's also a metacognitive view that helps them achieve growth.

The bottom line is that our students, groups, or mentees must first know that we care. You can fill in the blank: *"People don't care how much you know until they know ___ ___ ___ ___ "* [how much you care]. This idea is paramount. Hold it as you begin.

## Start with Humility.

As you begin conducting mentoring conversations, remember to start with humility. Yes, you likely possess more experience (and perhaps years of life) than your mentee. You also have these conversation-starting tools to guide the process. One key point to remember is that you are beginning a journey in which *you* may learn new things and gain insights *from* your mentee that will help you personally grow and develop. Before engaging your mentee, ponder your own insights by reviewing the questions in each conversation. Consider your perspective and remind yourself to really listen to your mentee's responses. If you are open to these ideas, you may find yourself benefiting as much as your mentee. I hope this happens for you.

Everyone we have ever met and will ever meet knows something we do not know. If we, the mentors, are humbly open to that idea, our potential for impact increases greatly because we are diversifying our inputs and expanding *our* well of knowledge. Please re-read those last two sentences. They are foundational. They convey the most important idea in this book.

Here is a personal example of why we must start with humility. It came straight to my mind when I begin writing this section:

> If you ask anyone who grew up with younger siblings to describe how they felt about them early on, some might use the word irritating. That would have been my description of my little brother fifty years ago. But time provides perspective.

It is remarkable what can happen over the course of ten or twenty or fifty years. It turns out that little siblings become best friends. You might also realize that their rambunctiousness and energy evolve into determination and bravery. Some of the "worst" offenders—the most irritating—channel that energy and grow up to become first responders, or they serve in our military. Some become coaches or teachers or mentors, putting all that supposedly irritating energy to amazing use.

That's what my "irritating" little brother did. He dug in his heels and slowly put himself through college. Then for thirty-one years, he put his life on the line for people he did not know serving in the Portsmouth Fire Department. For the last fourteen years, he led that organization as Chief Bill Raison, and subsequently, began teaching and coaching as well. I could not be more proud of this formerly "irritating" little sibling. I have learned more from simply watching him than he will ever know.

So as you begin (or continue) your mentoring work, try to start with humility, realizing that every single person you encounter has potential beyond imagination (and as mentioned, know something you do not). Later in this book I talk about having conversations or mentoring people who are younger, older, or different from you in some manner. When we embrace differences with humility, we all stand to grow exponentially.

## Start with Yourself.

This book aims to help you become a better mentor. The best way to do that is to study (a bit) and grow personally, so we can then help others. Do you have a "learn list"? Those are items you wish to go learn sometime in the future. What are you reading? What podcasts do you tune in? As we grow, our potential to help others grows.

*Your Approach*

I have invested many years collecting ideas and bits of wisdom. You should see my file folder with hundreds of hand-written scribbles, many on napkins or scrap paper, and many written while driving down the road listening to a podcast or inspiring talk from a favorite leadership guru or pastor or speaker. In truth, I collected these ideas for myself. My desire was to improve *my own* approach and knowledge base so I could subsequently help others. Now, I have finally put everything together in one place so you, the reader, can have it as a ready resource, initially for your personal growth, and then to share with others as you become a better mentor.

To be transparent, this is a self-help book written for me. It is also written for you. Subsequently, it's a mentoring toolkit that will help you use your skills (bolstered by engaging conversation starters) to encourage growth and unimaginable potential in those you mentor.

I mentioned in the introduction that I have made notations in many of the outlines to emphasize the process — to explain what's happening behind the scenes. These sections, labeled as "Background" and "Metacognition Minder," provide this foundational information. I have done this for two reasons. First, so you, the reader, will see some of the theoretical framework and research behind the approaches. Secondly, (and most importantly) so you can personally grow and develop and gain insight that will then allow you to better engage in the conversations. Again, the more we learn and grow, the better we can help others.

*So, are you ready?*

Please turn to Conversation #1 and begin.

Section 3

# The 40 Conversations

# Conversations with Questions for Initiating Growth

 **Conversation #1**

### The Mentoring Launch Conversation

**Question Preview:** *If we did not know each other at all, what would you want me to know about you?*

**Purpose:** This outlines an introductory conversation to launch any mentoring relationship.

**Background:** Developing a successful mentoring relationship must begin with two foundational pieces. We must get to know each other more deeply (beyond basic superficial or transactional interactions), and we must develop goals (individual and joint) for the time we are investing. Many formal mentoring relationships begin with a one-sided or prescribed goal. This is a tactical error that can result in missing some of the most beneficial and critical elements of the relationship.

When we co-construct the mentoring goal or goals, the relationship starts on a clear path. Along the way, we are provided with opportunities to pause, reflect, and evaluate progress. We have all heard, *"If you don't know where you're going, how will you know when you get there?"* We could expand that question to also ask, *"How will we know what to pack for the journey?"*

and *"What GPS, map, or pole star shall we follow?"* Talking it through at the outset will help you get started on the right path.

You have only two main questions for this conversation. But before jumping in, always start with a *connection before content* question. (You will read more about this idea from an engagement process guru I follow named Chad Littlefield in the chapters ahead.)

**Sample Initial Connection Questions:**

**What's your favorite food… and why?**
**What's something you want to learn… and why?**
**What is one of your favorite places… and why?**

These are a seemingly insignificant questions. Do we really care about someone's favorite food? Maybe, or maybe not. But food is not the point. Asking *why* something is a favorite food can transform a meaningless question or brief conversation into a connection. The *connection* is the critical component.

**Metacognition Minder:** The *why* is the most important piece. Do not miss this. Anytime we dig into someone's *why* we begin to discover what's below the surface. We begin to learn more about who someone is versus what they do or simply how they appear on the outside. These connections are foundational to the future mentoring or coaching relationship.

*Why* questions provide glimpses of that which matters most in someone's life. They also help the person answering to reflect, clarify, and sometimes remember (or return to the forefront of their mind) things that are most important. Busyness stifles our thinking and kills our clarity. We are sidetracked to the point of wasting hours, days, and even years on things that are not core to what we value, what we want to do, or where we want to go.

So, back to our question. Asking *"Why is that your favorite food?"* may sound unimportant, but the answer may begin to provide insight into what is important in a person's life. We all have diverse backgrounds and histories and cultural ways of understanding our world. Discovering someone's *why* behind a favorite food might surprise you and might offer a connection you would have missed.

**The Discussion:** Here are your conversation questions.

**Question 1:**

>  **If we did not know each other at all, what would you want me to know about you?**

I borrowed this question directly from the national award-winning photographer and author, John Noltner who uses it in his work building community and bridging divides across the country. You can learn more about that mission (and be inspired) at A Peace of My Mind (http://apomm.net).

I suggest deploying a teaching tactic here called "Think. Write. Share." Each person (mentor and mentee) should invest five minutes to think about what they might want to share, jotting some bullet points on a scrap of paper or on your phone. Finally, commence sharing.

This may feel a bit awkward, but it allows everyone time to process prior to jumping into conversation. For the quieter folks (some might label as introverted), it allows them time to process and curate what they want to share. For the more vocal folks (extraverted, rambunctious, and perhaps over-caffeinated), it forces them (me included) to pause for a moment and truly reflect on the process, the potential for the relationship, and what is most important (versus just jumping in without a plan or path as I have often done in life).

Once you have shared some basics, take the time to follow trails of joint interests or geographies. Be curious. Let me repeat that one: **Be curious.**

Then, move on to the second question.

**Question 2:**

>  **What are our individual and joint goals for this time we are investing?**

On the surface, this question sounds heavy duty, but don't let it weigh down the conversation too much. The goals for today are just to get started. They may shift and change completely over time. That's okay, and it is a natural occurrence. So no worries there. For today, simply name one or two ideas that come to mind about what you and your mentee want to achieve during your upcoming talks.

Some mentee examples might include:

- to gain insight and wisdom on my career
- to have a sounding board for advice on life issues

Some mentor examples might include:

- to provide insight and wisdom
- to learn from the mentee (Remember, everyone you meet knows things you do not know.)

Jointly, you both may simply wish to have a pleasant time together with predictable occurrences (setting a recurring date to meet), and to enjoy the opportunity for personal and professional development.

**Summary:** This conversation should lead to some connections and to your individual and joint goals for the relationship. If you stall or run out of points to share (a normal thing that happens), do not worry. Jump into one of the prompting questions below.

**Stalled Conversation Prompting Questions:**

**Un-stall Question 1:**

What is a favorite memory from your childhood?

This is a reflective question. Its aim is to start an appreciative inquiry (hence the qualifier "favorite") in your mentee's brain. When they finish their story (and if time allows), prompt them with this: *"Tell me more."*

**Un-stall Question 2:**

What do you hope the future holds for you?

This is a future focused question. It is broad by design at this early stage in the formation of the mentoring relationship. Again, after they share, prompt them to *tell you more.*

**Follow-up:** Ask your mentee how they felt about the conversation. Set the date and time for your next meeting. Also set a deadline to complete any exercise or handout, homework, further reading or video/podcast, if applicable. For this conversation, I might suggest writing down your goal statements and then reviewing them from time to time. If they shift, simply note any changes, additions, or deletions, and remember, fluidity is okay.

## Conversation #2

### The Being Remembered Conversation

**Question Preview:** *What do you want people to say about you when you're gone from this earth?* (i.e., *How do you want to be remembered?*)

**Purpose:** Though this is a deep question, touching on it early is important because this gets at the ultimate mentoring aim: *helping people (and groups) consider their life purpose and mission.*

**Background:** This is a rephrase of the classic Steven Covey question from *The 7 Habits of Highly Effective People*. It is one of the most powerful questions one can ever ponder. (Note: Versions of it will show up in the *Bucket List* and *Personal Mission* conversations later in this book. This is intentional.) Throughout recorded history, people have pondered the question of life's purpose.

At this early stage in your mentoring relationship, you can simply touch on this one. There is no need to go deep, yet. It is a definite brain engager because we are often too busy to pause and reflect in this way. So for most, the question will linger for a while.

**The Discussion:** Simply ask this conversation's question.

>  **What do you want people to say about you when you're gone from this earth?**
> **(i.e., How do you want to be remembered?)**

Remember to listen with intention to really hear and learn about your mentee. Be curious. Ask any naturally occurring prompting questions that come to mind, including my favorite, *"Could you tell me more?"*

**Follow-up:** Ask your mentee how they felt about the conversation. Set the date and time for your next meeting. You might suggest having your mentee jot down a few words or phrases to answer this question. This will begin preparing them for the *Personal Mission* challenge.

 **Conversation #3**

## 5 Things to Have, Do, Help, and Be: A Personal Futuring Exercise

**Question Preview:** *"Who do you want to become?"*

**Purpose:** This exercise can help those you mentor envision and create the future they desire. It challenges them to think in distinct but related categories, triangulating to lead them to action.

**Background:** Everyone… every company, every non-profit, etc. has two options for the future. These are the one that ***will*** be if we do nothing and continue the status quo or the one that ***could*** be if we work to achieve it by planning and acting to reach desired ends, goals, dreams, mission. Peter Drucker said it best, *"The best way to predict the future is to create it."*

**The Discussion:** Remind your mentee that most people are asked at an early age, *"What do you want to be when you grow up?"* We often prompt young minds with examples: *"Do you want to be a firefighter? A teacher? A farmer?"*

What if the more important question is: **"Who do you want to become?"** This is qualitatively different. This is perhaps the best question to ask to prompt future thinking, focus, and goal setting.

Use the chart below as a guide or template. In your mentoring meeting, simply divide a blank paper into fourths, write "5 things I want…" at the top, and then write one prompt (to have… to do… to help… to be…) in each quadrant. Give your mentee time to jot down one or two items in each box as you discuss them. When completed, challenge them to carry this around, think, reflect, and update it over the next few weeks. Reflection over time is powerful. Afterward, suggest they discuss insights with a trusted friend or family member.

### *What are 5 things you want...*

| **...to have:** (These can be tangible or intangible.) | **...to do:** (This is about *what* you might do: jobs, career, things for fun, Bucket List items, etc.) |
|---|---|
| **...to help:** (These can be big and small. Think broadly.) | **...to be:** (Not *what* you might do, but *who* you might become.) <br><br> **Challenge:** (List actions that will move you toward your *who*.) <br><br> 1. <br><br> 2. |

**Analysis:** *[This is written as if you are speaking to your mentee.]*

Look at the things you want **to have** and **to help**. Really consider them. Now, will the things you want **to do** move you in the right direction to accomplish them in the future? If not, add to the *To Do List*, then prioritize it. You cannot do everything. Another strategy here is to put some broad target dates next to your **to do** items (e.g., in five years). This can help.

**Challenge Activity:** *[Again, written as example wording you might say directly.]*

The *To Be* category will reflect how people remember you, now or when you're gone. (i.e., When someone thinks of you, what pops into their mind?) So consider two action items that will help you accomplish **who you want to be** and *how* you want to be remembered. Some may be short-term actions, some long-range. *For example:* If you want to be remembered as someone who was/is kind, what do you need to start doing to accomplish that? Jot down one or two things.

**Follow-up:** Ask your mentee how they felt about the conversation. Set the date and time for your next meeting. With this experiment in particular, have them carry this paper around for a couple of weeks to review, reflect, or make adjustments.

**Mentor challenge:** Do this activity yourself. Think about these questions. Ask yourself if you are taking action to accomplish things most important to your life goals.

## Conversation #4

### The Bucket List

**Question Preview:** *Do you have a Bucket List?*

**Purpose:** To help your mentee continue and deepen their thinking about what matters most in life.

**The Discussion:** Simply ask the person you are mentoring this seemingly unimportant question.

**Do you have a Bucket List?**

How often do you spend a little time thinking about (or pursuing) items on your bucket list? Do you even have one? Most of us have some things we'd like to do or accomplish in life. Some of us write a formal list on paper. Others have a list in their head. Often, the bucket list resides in our personal lives, but having one in our professional lives can make us more effective leaders as well.

Before we explore that, do you realize that by definition and logic that if you have a bucket list, you're thinking about dying? That may seem morbid, but it is in fact a good thing to think about what you want to do before you die.

**The Detail:** [Feel free to read this paragraph aloud to your mentee.]

In their 2016 *Book of Joy*, the Dalai Lama and Bishop Desmond Tutu instruct us to consider our own mortality. They rightly contend that this will bring a sense of urgency, perspective, and gratitude. Author and pastor Andy Stanley (2014a) similarly tells us that, *"priority determines capacity."* He points to an ancient Jewish text (Psalm 90) that says, *"teach us to number our days"* in order to achieve wisdom. Numbering your days is thinking about how long you have to live — just as the bucket list has us thinking about specific things that we want to do while we're still alive. This can be powerful in helping us focus attention both at home and work.

Stanley also challenges us to *"compound our minutes"* (2014b), noting (my paraphrase):

1. There is a cumulative value to investing small amounts of time in certain activities over an extended period. (e.g., exercise; spending time with family; mentoring a new coworker or student)
2. Neglect is also cumulative. (e.g., *not* exercising; *not* doing personal finances; *not* spending time with family; *not* sharing your life experiences; *not* fulfilling leadership opportunities when they arise)
3. There is no cumulative value to the random things we opt for over the important things. (e.g., surfing the internet; micromanaging instead of delegating)

If we're attentive to the limited time we have, we can use it more effectively. In turn, we can accomplish things that really matter. As mentors and leaders, we must simultaneously model this approach and behavior for others.

**Summary:** So how does all this come together?

Do you want to get more done? Do you want to increase your capacity? Make a bucket list. Try having one for home (personal life) and one for work (professional life). Write down those items that are most important — ones you really want to accomplish. Then, start numbering your days. Follow the advice of the Dalai Lama, Bishop Tutu, and Andy Stanley. Consider your mortality. I think you'll be glad you did.

**Ask your mentee to think about one or two items from their bucket lists that they could begin to tackle in the next couple of days or weeks?**

- **Personal Bucket List**
- **Professional Bucket List**

**Challenge them to think about how these might help their career, personal life, their studies, or even their family.**

For this conversation, remember that whether you are mentoring someone, teaching a class, or leading a team, challenge them with this question. If you participate as well, there is a bonus: you might have some fun and increase *your* available time for checking off one or two of *your* bucket-list items.

**Follow-up:** Ask your mentee how they felt about the conversation. For this activity, challenge them to write their Bucket List down. Then, ask them to write five (5) things they could stop doing that would free-up time for important items. Set the date and time for your next conversation. *Ask them to bring these lists.*

**Mentor challenge:** Do this activity yourself. Think about these questions. Write a personal and professional bucket list.

## For additional reference / reading:

Dalai Lama XIV, Desmond Tutu, and Douglas Carlton Abrams. *The Book of Joy: Lasting Happiness in a Changing World.* New York: Avery, 2016.

Stanley, Andy (Nov. 15, 2014). *Time Of Your Life 2 - At Capacity.* Available at: https://youtu.be/mIsnLZqmk_4

Stanley, Andy (Nov. 15, 2014). *Time Of Your Life 3 - Compounding Minutes.* Available at: https://youtu.be/YomJ6TUXChM

 ## Conversation #5

### The Values Review

**Question Preview:** *What matters most? How do your values affect your decision making?*

**Key Objectives:** To help your mentees think about what is most important in life.

**Introduction:** As individuals, we all have varying values and belief systems. We come from differing backgrounds and places. This gives us a rich and beautiful diversity. But how do we incorporate values into our everyday work? How do we ensure our core values are the fundamental beliefs that guide behavior and action?

It might be helpful to photocopy the chart below to share with those you mentor. (Note: this is a great classroom or group exercise as well.) Ask participants to review the generic *values* words below. Consider their personal connection to each.

**Instructions:**

1. Put a checkmark by items that you feel are important to you. Check as many as you want.
2. Narrow the checked items down to your Top 10 most important values. Underline these; but do not rank them.
3. Then, narrow to your Top 5 values. Circle these.
4. Lastly, rank the circled items in order from 1 (most important) to 5 (less important).

| Career | Respect | Cooperation | Popularity |
|---|---|---|---|
| Happiness | Freedom | Honesty | Fitting in |
| Service | Justice | Friendship | Pride |
| Courage | Fairness | Self-discipline | Loyalty |
| Love | Generosity | Responsibility | Community |
| Diversity | Compassion | Sharing | Progress |
| Perseverance | Beauty | Individuality | Spiritual / Faith |
| Reason | Patience | Prosperity | Wealth |
| Ambition | Creativity | Education | Family |
| Intelligence | Play | Belief | Tradition |
| Inclusion | Kindness | _____ | _____ |

**Questions to consider about your values:**

1. Why do we need to know, name, and talk about our core values?
2. Who or what influenced your top values? (Consider family, society, geography, events.)
3. Have your top values changed over your lifetime? Will they? What might cause that?

**Questions to consider about other people and their values:**

1. What happens when you need to work with someone whose values differ from yours?
2. Have you ever suppressed or temporarily ignored your values to fit in? (Or get a job? Etc.)

3. Can you respect someone who holds a fundamentally opposite value from you?

**Follow-up:** Look around for something that represents what is important to you. Perhaps it is something in nature, a quote, a sign, a person, or a pattern or design. Reflect on how that represents one of your core values this week, and then share it at the next meeting.

**Mentor challenge:** Do this activity yourself. Think about your most important values. Consider the questions too.

# Conversation #6

## Your Personal Mission

**Question Preview:** *What is your mission in life?*

**Purpose:** To help your mentee continue to deepen their thinking about what matters most in life, and to officially write it down in a personal mission statement.

**Background:** I assembled this exercise from numerous activity guides that have been used for years by myself and colleagues at Ohio State University Extension. I added the "2 Words" feature to challenge folks to boil everything down to the basics and to provide something easy to remember for daily guidance. Perhaps this sounds too simplistic, but I challenge you to give it a try. Being missional gives you priorities. Priorities let you say "no" to non-essentials, increasing capacity. Capacity provides options that enhance living.

**The Discussion:** *What is a personal mission? Who needs one?* A personal mission is a statement about your *why*. This is what drives you to get out of bed in the morning. It describes what you believe is most important in life, what you wish to focus on, and what you want to be known for. If you allow it to direct your thoughts and actions each day, it has the *potential* to improve your life.

I often tell my students to consider holding on to this paper. When one finds themself applying for a promotion or future job, having *(and referencing)* a personal mission can help them stand out from other candidates. Many graduate school applications request a personal philosophy and/or mission statement as well. This can be an excellent start.

[It may be helpful to photocopy this exercise to share with those you mentor.]

**4 Steps to Your Personal Mission:**

1. Think about your **Core Beliefs and Values.** Write down 4 or 5 key words or phrases under each of the following.

Core beliefs: What are some key things you believe?

Core values: What are some key things you value?

*Overall, what really matters in life? What's <u>most important</u>?*

2. **Hopes, Dreams, Desires, Goals:** Think about your hopes, dreams, desires, and goals. Do not limit these based on current circumstances. Jot down 2 or 3 items under each category. These can be whatever comes into your mind. These are not commitments but *possibilities*.

Personal:

School/Career:

Community/World:

Family/Friends:

Spiritual:

3. **Leaving a Legacy:** These questions are to help focus your thinking.

How would you like to be remembered? What one thing do you want people to say about you (now or after you're gone)?

What have you contributed to the world during your life so far? What do you dream of contributing in the future?

What steps can you begin to take to achieve your desired contributions, hopes, dreams, and goals?

**4. Drafting Personal Mission Statement:**

Review everything you've written so far. Circle or <u>underline</u> any words that stand out in your mind.

You are now ready to write your Personal Mission Statement using key words and ideas from above. Don't worry about getting it perfect. Just get down the basics. Include the most important ideas and words. You may refine it later, and it will evolve over time. That's okay. For now, write a brief draft—one sentence or phrase. You could begin with: *My mission in life is to…*

✎ _____

_____

_____

_____

**You in 2 Words:**

You now have a DRAFT mission. Try to quantify what it says in just two words. What are the two most important words that could define you?

1. _____ 2. _____

The signature line below is meaningful. It conveys the seriousness of missional living. *Sign your name. Then live it.*

Signed: _____ Date: _____

**Summary / Final Action Step:**

Challenge your mentee. As they complete the exercise, ask whether their friends, co-workers, and family members know these things about them. How might they begin to let others see and understand what is most important in their life? How might they share their newly written mission with others? Jot ideas down. *Then do them.*

**Follow-up:** For this conversation, I recommend asking your mentee to take the paper home and think about it over the next few weeks. This is an exercise that should be revisited until they hone it down to a final version.

Set the date and time for your next conversation. Set a deadline to complete the mission.

**Mentor challenge:** Do this activity yourself. Write a personal mission that you can follow.

 **Conversation #7**

## Leveraging Gratitude

**Question Preview:** *Can increasing gratitude improve your brain chemistry and help you feel better? Can it help your career?*

**Purpose:** To help your mentee understand how practicing gratitude can make a major difference in their internal thought process, and how that can help their career.

**Background:** The science of gratitude has expanded greatly in the past twenty years. Studies increasingly show that regularly practicing gratitude contributes to better relationships, decreased anxiety, and increased internal satisfaction. These bolster what Daniel Goleman labels emotional and social intelligence, key items for success in our careers and lives.

These were once labeled *soft skills*. But I regularly talk with employers who want to hire our OSU graduates that are in possession of both technical knowledge and what I call **critical skills**—teamwork, communication, leadership, mission focus, curiosity, and others. Gratitude is high on that list as well.

When we pause to focus on things we're grateful for, we activate the prefrontal cortex in our brains and release important neurochemicals that help give us feelings of reward, bonding, and understanding. When we shift our thinking from negative to positive, there is a positive surge that can energize and reinvigorate us even on a bad day.

> ***My example:*** *I still teach one undergraduate class at Ohio State. Each semester, I challenge my students to keep a gratitude list. I ask them to jot down five (5) items each week. I check in periodically to see how they're doing. Each time, when they share an item or two, the entire room brightens. The energy is palpable. Everyone is lifted. It is an amazing thing.*

**The Discussion:** How might we increase our practice of gratitude? This may sound very simple, but we need only write down three things for which we're grateful for 21 days in a row. Writer and former Harvard researcher, Shawn Achor, says practicing gratitude for 21 days will train our brains to look at the world differently. Once the habit is formed, we start scanning the world for positives instead of threats. It's a game changer.

Researcher Robert Emmons, likewise, said that even though we do not have total control over our emotions, *"being grateful is a choice that can sustain us through the ups and downs of our lives."* When we become more grateful, we are more stress resistant and our self-worth increases. This often shows outwardly. And again, when that is noticed, it can result in career progression and success.

Ask your mentee these gratitude questions:

 **Are you willing to take the 21-day gratitude test? (i.e., Will you write three things per day that you're grateful for?)**

— Yes? — No?

**How might increasing gratitude help your career? (Make a list of ideas on this as well.)**

Here are some additional thoughts around gratitude, along with some ideas to try at the office:

1. Start your next meeting with a gratitude question. For example:
   a. Name a project you're thankful to be working on.
   b. Name a work colleague and tell how you're grateful for them.
   c. What is a recent lesson you have learned, and how are you thankful for it?

2. In work situations, think about how you can be grateful for the person, not just their output.

3. Gratitude and appreciation go hand-in-hand. Review Dr. Gary Chapman's *5 Languages of Appreciation* (https://www.appreciationatwork.com/). Consider folks with whom you work, and how they prefer to receive gratitude. How might you show gratitude and appreciation for them this week?

**Summary:** Challenge your mentee(s) to start and maintain a gratitude list. Keep it simple so it's not a chore. Ask them to share an item or two with you at your next meeting. Observe what happens when they (or anyone) shares something for which they're grateful.

## For additional reference / reading:

Dr. Gary Chapman's *5 Languages of Appreciation* (https://www.appreciationatwork.com/)

# Conversation #8

## Building Curiosity

**Question Preview:** *What are you curious about?*

**Purpose:** To help your mentee understand that focusing on their curiosity can lead to learning, which is a major predictor of success.

**The Discussion:** *What are you curious about?* Some folks will respond to this question with an immediate answer: *"Everything!"* Others may just look at you and ask what you mean. Whether at one end of the spectrum, or somewhere in the middle, watching someone respond to this question will allow you to immediately know a lot about them and their potential for long-term success.

In brief, curiosity is one of the most important traits and a high predictor for success identified by researchers at Korn Ferry, an international business consulting firm. In CEO Gary Burnison's Special Edition, *The Fall Whisper*, he says most people think of growth, strategy, and vision as key traits for leaders. But curiosity has recently become recognized as an absolutely critical piece.

Since the pandemic of 2020, Burnison says our world has experienced *"nonstop ambiguity"* which requires leaders to look at the world with an open mind. Whatever your organization (for profit, non-profit, education, government, etc.), today's rapid changes can only be met if we are aware of emerging trends and subsequently ready ourselves for action to meet the opportunities (or the risks) presented. We can meet this challenge by increasing our curiosity.

Here are three questions that can help increase curiosity:

> **What are you curious about right now?**
>
> **How might you increase your curiosity (in more areas of your work and life)?**
>
> **Might listening be a strategy for increasing your curiosity? (Think about that one for a few moments.)**

Think about context. Burnison says context is best friends with curiosity. By considering context, almost any event, trend, or observation can be handled or reframed to help visualize a path forward. By pairing curiosity with context and perspective, we can determine action.

**Summary:** In cultivating your curiosity, don't forget to expand your knowledge (and possible options) further by remembering to listen well. The saying about *"experts not listening because they already know the answer"* rings true here. Imagine what might be missed if we are not open and curious to hear and learn about the other opportunities out there.

**Follow-up:** Ask your mentee to create a list of some ways they might increase their curiosity. Challenge them to consider how listening might be a powerful strategy as well.

## For additional reference / reading:

Burnison, Gary (October 9, 2022). *The Fall Whisper.* Korn Ferry special edition publication.

# Conversations with Questions for Deepening Connections

 **Conversation #9:**

### From Why? to What?

**Purpose:** To help your mentee change their perspective.

**Question Preview:**

>  When bad news hits, can you change the question in your head from, "Why is this happening?" to "What can I learn?"

**The Discussion:** Either share my story below or (better yet) share a similar story of your own with your mentee.

> **My story:**
>
> *"I am sorry Mr. Raison. You have cancer."*
>
> I heard nothing after that.
>
> It was August 2014. I had gone in for a routine colonoscopy having hit the magical age of fifty. Outpatient screenings

had become quite accessible and recommended. But at fifty, I knew how these things were supposed to go. If they find anything slightly suspicious, the doctor says, *"We found a small spot and have sent it out to the lab for a biopsy. We'll not even call unless there's a reason for a follow-up test."*

Right? No doctor ever just walks in the room, sits down, looks you in the eye, and says, *"I'm sorry. You have cancer."* That's not how it works. Or so I thought.

It's remarkable how many things can run through your mind in an instant. There is an explosion of thoughts... pictures of those you love... of your hopes and dreams... of questions like, *"How long do I have?"* This time is often protracted and worsened by Googling things likes, "colon cancer survival rates" (which I would NEVER recommend doing). After a few hours of settling down, one question emerges and lingers:

***"Why is this happening to me?"***

This is a legitimate question, and I think it is natural to ask it. It is also dangerous to remain in that space. Asking *why* does nothing helpful because *there is no answer.* Cancer happens.

And guess what? Job loss happens. As does stress. Emotional breakdown. Pain. Death. Or how about criticism? That can be extraordinarily painful. Write your own list. Better yet, don't. Instead, see if you can reframe the question and your thinking.

**The Switch:**
When faced with a major life challenge or pain point, here is one of the most powerful things a person can do:

 **Instead of asking: "Why is this happening?"**
**Ask, "What can I learn?"**

As a mentor, if you can help someone shift their response from *why* to *what*, you can change their life for the better.

**The Final Challenge:**
Okay. If you have decided (or convinced your mentee) to try and do this intellectual shift the next time you experience a significant pain or stress point, you are to be applauded. Now, I hate to tell you this, but don't stop there.

Here's the final challenge. Change the question from *"Why is this happening?"* to *"What can I learn?"* Then, ask yourself:

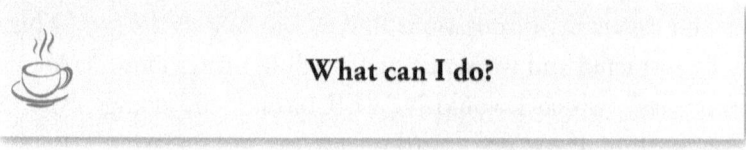

It's okay to take some time with this question. For my cancer diagnosis, they *told* me what to do. Make an immediate appointment with a surgeon and an oncologist. We did that. [Note my shift from "me" to "we." Here, my spouse became an integral part of the process to help me make these decisions.] After a local consultation that described a tried-and-true surgical procedure, we decided to get a second opinion from a teaching/research hospital, the James Cancer Center at The Ohio State University where I work. There, we learned about a less invasive procedure that had the same success rate with far fewer side effects and/or lifestyle changes.

*What could we do?* We took action, educated ourselves, and made a decision for the second option which, today, finds me still cancer-free after almost ten years.

*What else can you do?* Share your burden. Talk with friends. Make an appointment with a counselor. They can help greatly. In my case, along with the second opinion, we also took action to lower our mental stress by leaning into our family's faith tradition and ancient wisdom literature. Here, we found a different, but significant *why*. If interested, please see the text inset, **Other Action: Leaning on Faith in My Cancer Journey,** below.

**Follow-up with your mentee:** Assign some homework on this one. Ask your mentee to watch for a *why* question to hit their mind in the next couple of weeks. Challenge them to really pay attention. It need not be a life-altering event, but watch for a stressor or trigger point. It could be something small like being nearly out of gas and discovering the price just went up by forty cents! Or it could be that their coffee pot quit working.

When they encounter the trigger-event (at work, home, or play), *have them text you the very moment they change the question in their head from Why to What.* Assure them you REALLY want to know when it's happening. Compelling your mentee to take immediate action on this experiment will help to cement this as a habit in their brain.

This is powerful stuff. I hope you will give it a try.

### Other Action: Leaning on Faith in My Cancer Journey

*[Hundreds of research studies show positive mental and physical health benefits in people with a faith tradition. Please see the conversation on Faith which appears later in this book for more on that topic.]*

When I got home from that early morning appointment and unexpected cancer diagnosis, my head was still reeling from the doctor's words. I was still asking, *"Why?"* while I was locked in one of those existential moments. I wondered if I would get to grow old with my spouse or see our young daughters grow up. I also wondered how I personally would handle the challenge. Would I be scared? Angry? Victimized? Defeated? It was an unbelievable weight.

Fortunately, I thought to look for answers or guidance in my faith tradition which is rooted in the difficult teaching of practicing gratitude, loving everyone, being humble, and giving of yourself and your resources to help others. As documented in both Biblical and other historical texts, this way of living was suggested over 2,000 years ago by a Jewish rabbi called Jesus. Though tremendously challenging, some find this way of life quite fulfilling.

So in my search for hope or to find the meaning of getting cancer, I consulted these ancient Biblical texts. They yielded two passages that became immediately helpful. As I studied them, I realized they may be applicable to anyone who is having a difficult time. The first passage is from an early writer, James the Just, who posits (my unofficial paraphrase):

> *Consider it pure joy whenever you face trials because this tests your faith to produce perseverance. Perseverance will make you mature and complete, not lacking anything.*
> (roughly excerpted from James 1:2-4)

That's quite an idea and an extraordinary promise. But I wondered if it could really be true. Could this *trial* of having cancer make me stronger, more *complete*? Wow. What a thought. I guess the modern version is, *"Whatever doesn't kill you makes you stronger."*

These ideas helped me slowly begin shifting my thinking. At the end of August, I had a successful surgery. When I got home after eight days of recovery in the hospital, I was reading *The Message* (Eugene Peterson's paraphrase of the Bible). In Paul's second letter to the early church at Corinth, he claims (my unofficial paraphrase):

> *...we should not regret distress that drives us to God. That kind of pain can turn us around and make us more alive, more concerned, more sensitive, more reverent,*

*more human, more passionate, more responsible.* (roughly excerpted from 2 Corinthians 7: 10-13)

What? Distress is helpful? Yes. There is a lot written on this phenomenon in the transformational leadership theory research literature. Major life events and/or stressors can help us focus and truly become more alive. Writers and philosophers from Steven Covey, Rick Warren, the 14th Dalai Lama, and John Lennon have paraphrased this same idea, challenging us to *get busy living.*

So whether you have a faith tradition or not, you (or your mentee) may find support, wisdom, and hope in any number of these remarkable commentaries and writings. I urge you to look at texts from multiple sources. Many faiths offer wonderful ideas that can bolster our mental outlook which in turn, helps our physical healing.

Whether cancer or criticism, we experience trials and distresses every day. The secret is to reframe our thinking. If you are post-cancer like me, living with it today, or just having a hard time right now, I hope you will remember this: *We can learn a lot when we struggle. We can grow exponentially through trials. We can lean on each other.* And perhaps a faith tradition will help as well.

The secret is simple: Change the question from Why? to What?

# Conversation #10

## Helping Your Mentees Feel Safe

**Question Preview:** *Do you feel like you can be yourself in our mentoring conversations? Have I, as the mentor, demonstrated my own mistakes and imperfections?*

**Purpose:** This conversation aims to equip you with some background information that can help you understand why mentees need to feel safe, and how you can help facilitate that comfort.

**Background:** In his 2014 TED talk, *Why Good Leaders Make You Feel Safe*, Simon Sinek cites numerous anecdotal stories of how leaders build trust and accomplish missions by making their people feel safe. I re-watched Sinek's talk while thinking about how it parallels teaching, coaching, and mentoring, particularly when we shifted to online instruction during the initial COVID-19 crisis in 2020. Today, online instruction and mentoring continue, hence my inclusion of this module.

Pause for a moment and consider the people you're leading, coaching, teaching, or mentoring. Do they feel safe, right now in whatever living or work situation they find themselves? Really consider these folks: *How are they doing right now?*

Think back to Maslow's hierarchy of needs. From the bottom and moving upward, the needs are physiological, safety, love and belonging, esteem, and self-actualization. Do all our charges have their physiological needs met? Has their home situation changed post-COVID? Have they (or a parent or partner) recently lost a job? Are they worried about paying their cell phone bill?

If (and that's a big if) their physiological needs are mostly met, Maslow posits *safety* as the second-most foundational factor. Hence my question: Do our mentees feel safe in a conversation with us? Will they attempt a response to any question posed? Or are they cautious? Have you, as the mentor, demonstrated your own mistakes and reassured them this is how we learn and grow?

| Maslow's Hierarchy of Needs | |
|---|---|
| Self-actualization | Creativity, morality, problem solving, acceptance of facts, lack of prejudice |
| Self-esteem | Confidence, achievement, fulfillment |
| Love and belonging | Family, friendship, intimacy, connection |
| Safety and security | Physical (bodily) security, work, resources, morality, family, health |
| Physiological needs | Physical needs (air, water, food, sleep, reproduction, etc.) |

Here is an example I almost always use when I am teaching courses on campus.

### My Vulnerable Opening Lecture

For years, I have opened my graduate level courses by asking students, *"Why are you in here? Have you not heard about my horrible reputation for marking up papers?"* I then share examples of my feedback on the screen:

*"This paper needs help from someone who knows how to write."* And, *"I see this paper as less significant given the paucity of data to inform the conclusions."*

Then, I ask what they think. *"Is this a bit harsh?"* I tell them I think it might be. But finally, like Paul Harvey of yesteryear, I deliver the rest of the story. I share that this is not feedback I have given students, but it's feedback **I have received** in the past. I get lots of surprised looks at this point! I can hear the questions in their heads. *"What? Dr. Raison can't write?"* Then, I very clearly state:

*"I'm going to be tough on your papers because I want you to learn in the safety of this class. I do not want you to EVER*

*experience this. It's a punch in the gut. It hurts. And I want you to avoid that."*

I do then share that *I used these experiences* to improve my writing, and subsequently have been successful in publishing, grant writing, achieving tenure and promotion to the rank of full professor at a Tier 1 research university. *"So I'm not a total loser,"* I note. That breaks the tension, and they laugh. Most of the graduate students also see me differently. They tell me they feel comfortable approaching me and asking what they may previously have labeled a "stupid question."

Safety, trust, and authenticity matter. As I have noted before, you must *reach before you teach*. This is the same in mentoring.

Continuing with Maslow, once physiological and safety needs are generally met, they no longer dominate and no longer drive behavior. Other higher-order needs grow. For example, upper-level needs, *love and belonging (social aspects of life) and esteem,* may become even more important in triggering mentorship participation.

As noted, stresses from physical social isolation can be debilitating. Could adding a five-minute low risk opening question at the beginning of each mentoring session enhance connections and progress? I think so. Here's an approach.

**The Discussion:** Ask your mentee these questions.

> **Do you feel like you can be yourself in our mentoring conversations?**
> **Have I, as the mentor, demonstrated my own mistakes and imperfections?**

Sharing shortfalls, being transparent and authentic, and demonstrating humility goes a long way in a mentoring relationship. And the road should run both directions. This is how we learn and grow.

**Reflection:** Take just a moment to think about why you became a mentor. Was it because you were inspired by someone who mentored you? Did someone tell you that you would make a good mentor? For most of us, we do this because we care deeply about people. We are energized by them. We find hope for the future in them.

**Summary:** This week, try to use one of these ideas to help your mentee feel safe. Give them some grace. Give yourself grace too. Some of these ideas can help your mentoring work result in great progress toward personal and professional goals.

Above all, remember to encourage your mentees to keep a check on their mental health, and seek help when needed. Then, borrowing from Sinek, consider how you as the mentor can help your folks feel safe.

**Follow-up:** Ask your mentee how they felt about the conversation. After this conversation, have them watch Sinek's 2014 TED talk (referenced below).

## For additional reference / reading:

Sinek, Simon (2014). Why good leaders make you feel safe. TED2014.

 ## Conversation #11

## What's Your Biggest Fear? A Check-in for Mental Health

**Question Preview:** *What's your biggest fear? What would you tell a friend who shared these worries with you?*

**Purpose:** This conversation aims to help you engage your mentee about the topic of mental health without explicitly pointing to mental health. Like many of these conversations, it aims to create an internal *ah-ha moment* and equip them with an additional tool. In this case, it simply suggests asking one question to help your mentee reframe any issue and *see it from another perspective.* This is one of the most powerful things a mentor can do.

**Background:** This is an experiment to try with those you mentor, coach, lead, supervise, or parent. It's written as a group exercise, but it also works well one-on-one. This conversation is in no way meant to serve as a counseling session. It is a deep question where a gentle approach can help our mentees remember or realize they may well already hold the answers or responses to some of their worries or anxieties.

Leaders encourage, inspire, and, according to author Simon Sinek, help their people *feel safe.* So how might we help people think through *and respond to* the anxieties and stresses they are feeling today?

**The Discussion:** For several years, I have done a classroom activity that is a kind of mental health check-in. This simple 10–20-minute exercise works with students and teams or can be modified for individual mentoring.

It begins by asking:

 **What's your greatest worry or biggest fear?**

Each semester, I ask my students to respond to this prompt anonymously using blank 3x5 index cards or via Poll Everywhere. When I first created this exercise about eight years ago, I regularly received a combination of serious and funny responses. Along with concerns about grades, family, and the future, students wrote, *"I'm afraid of spiders!" "Being eaten by a shark." "Vampires!"* In the past few years, I have received almost no funny responses whatsoever. All their responses are deeper concerns:

*"Not doing well in my classes this semester." "Never being enough." "Not being successful after college."*

*"Balancing my life." "The future." "Not living up to expectations." "Failure."*

I then share these anonymous responses. When students see what their classmates wrote, there is a visceral response—a collective but quiet acknowledgement on each face in the room. You can see it. You can feel it.

Then I ask this key question:

**What would you tell a friend who shared these worries with you?**

Each time I do this experiment, my students provide peer advice that is strengthening, encouraging, and hopeful. They have a remarkable ability to empathize and help each other. They have the answers!

**The critical piece:** Do not stop the conversation here. After your mentee or students share, follow up with the reflective learning piece:

**Why did we do this exercise?**

In every instance, my students immediately respond to this reflective *why* question with: *"It showed us that we're not alone." "We're not the only ones worried about stuff." "We can talk with friends and share our troubles."* Having them say and hear that reflection matters. It solidifies the lesson in real time.

**The Closing:** Restate how it is wonderful that they realize they have each other to lean on, and encourage them to do so. Then, ask the closing questions:

**What brings you comfort?**
**What brings you hope or joy?**

In my classes, students frequently respond: *"Family." "Talking with friends about my worries." "My dog." "Music." "My faith."*

I then summarize and emphasize their *comfort* responses and give them the following homework assignment:

> *"Acknowledge your concerns and worries. They are legitimate. Find a licensed counselor or a friend to talk with when you need. But also, invest time reflecting on those beautiful things that bring comfort. Life is good. You are not alone. We'll get through all of this… together."*

I hope you will give this experiment a try. It is a tremendously powerful reminder of how changing our perspective (from inward/self, to outward/other) can awaken insight and solutions.

**Follow-up:** Ask your mentee how they felt about this conversation. Set the date and time for your next meeting. For this conversation, ask them to watch for an opportunity to change their perspective by deploying the technique of, *"What would you tell a friend?"* when something bad happens. Let them know you would love if they shared it at your next meeting, but it is also okay if they don't.

## Conversation #12

### Bravery. Failure. Kindness.

**Question Preview:** *How were you brave today? How did you fail? How were you kind?*

**Purpose:** This conversation reminds us that bravery and failures occur every day, and that kindness is a mainstay which can be life changing for both the receiver and the giver.

**Background:** You are likely asking what bravery, failure, and kindness have in common, and how might a mentoring conversation around these items look. Your questions are appropriate and valid. These three seemingly disparate concepts were beautifully woven together in a 2016 Huffington Post article by a mom who was looking for meaningful conversations with her school-aged children. Hang in here with me please. This conversation can be life changing to older students and adults, as well as to someone you are mentoring.

In this article, author Meg Conley outlines the story of her concern with how to best help her children manage some of the struggles of youth. She came up with the idea of asking three questions:

- How can you be brave every day when facing an ever-changing world?
- How can you learn from failure and leverage that for later success?
- How can you be kind, even in the face of those who aren't so nice to you?

Notice anything? Yes. These questions are as germane to adults as they are to Conley's children. But in adulthood, our responses and the subsequent implications may have greater stakes and significance.

Conley's solution was found in asking the same three questions at their family dinner every night. How were you brave today? How were you kind? How did you fail? I have reordered them and changed the context for a mentoring conversation that has potential to capture attention and to be encouraging.

**The Discussion:** On the surface, these questions sound almost quaint. Perhaps even innocent. But they absolutely hold tremendous power. For more than five years now, I have been asking them at the start of one undergraduate course I teach here at Ohio State. And my students respond. On a couple of occasions, when I've jumped into a topic to start a class, they have stopped me and said, *"Wait! What about our brave, fail, kind questions?"* That always stops me short. I must ask myself, "What's *most important* here?" And I quickly remember: the students. I aim to encourage them to realize their highest potential. So I pause, and we share together how each of us experienced bravery, failure, and kindness in the preceding week.

Here are the questions. I suggest both mentee and mentor answer these together. Consider doing it every time you meet.

| 3 Questions for Reflection ||  |
|---|---|---|
| **Bravery:** | How were you brave today? | |
| **Failure:** | How did you fail today? | |
| **Kindness:** | How were you kind today? | |

**Question 1:** How were you brave today?

I expand this question to ask how can one be brave every day when facing challenges of work, home, finances, and an ever-changing world? The key here is to remember one thing: We are brave every day. Conley calls it a "legacy of bravery" that exists but is rarely considered in that light. That is, we are brave, but we do not name it and often we do not even recognize it. For some, getting out of bed is an act of bravery. Or it is making that appointment that you've been putting off. Maybe it is acknowledging a mistake or asking for forgiveness. Some things may seem relatively small, but deciding to act by being just a little brave can open paths for us. Take a moment right now. Consider something you did this week that was brave.

> *Bravery's Key Point:* We practice countless acts of bravery, but we do not hold them collective. If we can train our brains to recognize and remember small moments of bravery, we will have a tremendous tool (Archimedes' lever even) to deploy when something big happens. Like an athlete's muscle memory, this question equips us to deal with major life issues if and when needed.

**Question 2:** How did you fail today?

Again, I expand this question to ask how one can learn from failure and leverage that for later success. There are countless stories of inventors who considered failure as only data which compelled them to try new approaches until they found success. This can work for us as well.

> *Failure's Key Point:* As adults, we know that life is filled with failures. Some are self-inflicted. Recognizing and even calling those out can be powerful. Small failures are data, but so are the big ones. If we remember this, we can compel ourselves to keep trying. We can turn failure into a foundation, learning from and building on what did not work to subsequently find success.

In talking with her children, Conley says *"it is freeing to talk about the day's biggest debacles while eating grilled cheese and tomato soup."* As an adult, this approach sounds pretty good to me.

**Question 3:** How were you kind today?

This last question may seem out of place amid *bravery* and *failure*, but I think it fits well. As adults, we often experience similar challenges (like traumas) that we did in childhood. The question for us becomes: how can one be kind, even in the face of those who aren't so nice to you? This is a major challenge in life for many.

Conley says that often, *"society teaches our daughters that kindness is giving in or becoming weaker for others."* But that is incorrect for sons, daughters, or anyone. Conley says, *"kindness is leading with understanding and becoming stronger for others."* Wow. This is a truth we should encourage our mentees to consider and embrace.

> *Kindness's Key Point:* Kindness is a mainstay. When we practice it, it can be life changing for both the receiver and the giver.

**Metacognition Minder:** Many of the challenges of childhood have not changed. Try asking yourself these questions each day. Notice how you think about each question. Pay attention to how your brain and body respond. Which question results in a negative visceral reaction… one you wish you could dismiss? How might you accept what is? How might you endeavor to bravely move forward to *what could be*? We have these options in our childhood, but we do not have as much context in the form of life experience within which to situate a better response. As adults, these questions can be powerful reminders of what matters and of the potential we all possess.

**Follow-up:** Ask the person you are mentoring how they felt about the conversation. To help them cement the habit, challenge them to keep a list for one week of their bravery, failures, and kindness. They need not share it with you unless they wish. But this will help them practice the reflection.

Lastly, challenge your mentee and yourself to ask these questions at the end of every single day as a reflection or meditation. You too are brave in more ways than you know.

## For additional reference / reading:

Conley, M. (2016). *Brave, Kind, Fail: We Ask Our Kids the Same 3 Questions Every Night.* Huffington Post Online 08/24/2016. Available at: https://www.huffpost.com/entry/we-ask-our-kids-the-same-3-questions-every-night_b_11665530

## Conversation #13

### Joy vs. Happiness: Finding Fulfillment in Work and Life

**Question Preview:** *Could understanding the difference between happiness and joy help you survive unhappy moments in life (or undesirable job assignments at work)?*

**Purpose:** To help your mentee differentiate external, temporal happiness from internal, lasting joy.

**Background:** When was the last time you wished someone happy birthday? Or happy anniversary? Can you think of a song or two that has the word *happy* in the title or refrain? Our society is filled with artifacts that encourage us to pursue happiness. Heck, Thomas Jefferson included it in the U.S. Declaration of Independence. But what is the actual definition of being happy?

Dictionary.com suggests being *happy* is *"feeling or showing pleasure or contentment."* When I hear that, I think of a moment or an event. Generally, my mind does not generate the notion of long-term fulfillment. We have other words for those deeper contentment parts of life. I find an expanded meaning in words like fulfillment, satisfaction, and joy.

For *joy* in particular, I differentiate it as more of an internal feeling of satisfaction or contentment. I think of *happiness* as more of the external, temporary feeling of pleasure. Might differentiating these be helpful to your mentee?

**The Discussion:** Have you ever found yourself saying, *"I just want to be happy"*? That's legit. It's real. And at times, it is tangible, particularly after a long week. It doesn't seem like too much of a request. But if happiness is focused on more external, materialistic, or worldly pleasures, would it be better if we could shift our internal voice to say, *"I just want to have joy"*? Doing this moves us out of the temporal happiness into a long-term emotional well-being space.

Here are some related questions to for you and your mentee(s) to ponder:

**What does it mean to be happy?**

**Can you be unhappy, but still have joy?**

**Could understanding the difference between happiness and joy help you survive unhappy moments in life (or undesirable job assignments at work)?**

Discuss these for a bit. Find some examples from both of your lives. Maybe one of you had a mediocre annual evaluation in the past, and you remember how it definitely removed all happiness from you that day. Did you still like your job? Were you able to shift focus (maybe after a day or two) and reflect on how you could make some adjustments to improve the outcome at your next evaluation? Were you able to reflect on positive things in your life to counteract that momentary unhappiness?

Please note, this can be difficult to do. But practicing helps. Reflect on the Gratitude Conversation. Research shows when we practice thinking about positive things, we train our brains to default to more positive thoughts.

**Summary:** Though subtle and perhaps nuanced, joy and happiness can be thought of very differently. And when we do, we might just be able to get through those unhappy moments by leaning into our underlying joy which can endure hardship and trials, and point us to purpose.

I've quoted His Holiness the Dalai Lama and Archbishop Desmond Tutu (with Doug Abrams) in their 2016 *Book of Joy* noting that serving others is one of the best ways to achieve joy in life. In every mentoring conversation that I have, I try to talk about service. Serving others and offering encouragement are two of the greatest things we can do in life.

**Follow-up:** Ask your mentee what they think about differentiating happiness from joy. Challenge them to try shifting the conversation in their head the next time an unhappy event occurs and see if they can lean into underlying joy.

## For additional reading:

Dalai Lama XIV, Desmond Tutu, and Douglas Carlton Abrams. The Book of Joy: Lasting Happiness in a Changing World. New York: Avery, 2016.

**Conversation #14**

## Remembering to Listen (to Others and Yourself)

**Question Preview:** *Are you listening to respond or to truly understand? Are you listening to yourself?*

**Purpose:** This conversation starter has three parts. First, it reminds us (the mentors) to listen to hear and to understand versus listening to respond to what our mentees are saying. Secondly, our mentees need this as a reminder for their personal and professional growth and development. Finally, it challenges us to tune into our internal voice and consider our wellness across eight dimensions.

**Background:** How many times have you found yourself engaged in an individual (or even group) conversation in which you were ostensibly listening, but, in fact, found yourself going over exactly what you would say in response. You may have even been planning to interject, watching for the current speaker to pause or take a breath so you could jump in. Or worse, perhaps you have found your mind wandering completely away from the topic (and the actual speaker), not even hearing or acknowledging their words until they say, *"Did you even hear me?" "I just asked you a question."* Yikes. We are all guilty.

**The Discussion:** Below are some basic reminders about listening that can benefit everyone. Review these for yourself, then choose a couple to share with those you mentor.

**Listening to Others:** *Reminders on How to Listen for Understanding*

> **Attitude:** Check your stress levels. Smile. A deliberate attitude check can change any conversation. Remember: Let go of whatever worry or deadline you have looming. Focus on the person before you. And again, smile.

**Attend:** *Verbal attending* is when you practice intently listening without interruption, questions, or introducing new topics. *Physical attending* means providing a comfortable setting, having an *awareness* of the space you are occupying, and maintaining an open body posture. These are non-verbal clues that you care.

**Close reflection:** When mentoring (or participating in any conversation) if you can restate key ideas using the same words as much as possible, you show that you are closely listening and honoring their description of an event or concern. It can also show that you are honoring their history, background, or culture, further building connection and trust.

**Insightful reflection:** Look for ways to express the essential feelings that are said or hinted at. Be cautious in this approach, as you do not want to assume too much. *Use questions in your reflecting response to clarify or to go deeper.*

**Paraphrase:** Sometimes, restating your mentee's message in a summarized way can help. The main purpose is to see if you really understand, so your mentee can feel understood and encouraged to go on.

**Focus:** After listening, pause and take time to formulate a response that deliberately focuses on one aspect of your mentee's words. This can be done by picking out one word or a short phrase and repeating it. It may also be a question: *"You have been talking about several concerns. Which is most important to you?"*

**Summarize:** Put your mentee's key ideas and feelings together, and then invite them to respond. The second step is critical. You are making sure you have it right.

**Ask Open-Ended Questions:** After listening to understand, try asking an open-ended question to help you explore the situation. Open-ended questions cannot be answered with a yes or no. Be sure to begin with *how* or *what* to elicit a deeper response. Avoid *why* questions, as they may tend to sound accusatory and may put your mentee on the defensive.

**Listening to Others:** *The Art of Listening*

**Learn:** Listening is the most important communication tool. Ninety-eight percent of what we learn, we learn through our eyes and ears. Learning through the ears—listening—takes approximately forty-five percent of our time. If you are talking, guess how much you are not learning from someone else.

**Involve:** To be an effective listener, we must involve ourselves in the conversation. We show a *posture of involvement* including facing the person squarely, maintaining good eye contact, leaning forward and relaxing.

**Silence:** The effective use of silence during a conversation can be one of the most powerful ways to convey acceptance and encouragement. We typically fear silence because of the pressure we feel to do or say something. Silence also gives the speaker the opportunity to gather their thoughts and the courage to say what they want and need to say.

**Trust:** Without realizing it, the listener can fail the "trust test"—failing to offer support the speaker needs. The listener must avoid the pitfalls of argument, criticism, questioning, and phony reassurance. Effective listening depends on trust—demonstrating the understanding and acceptance of both the speaker's feelings and experiences.

**Empathy:** Empathy is the desire to understand and accept the thoughts, feelings, and positions of the other person. This does not mean the listener should have the same feelings and positions as the speaker, nor that you agree. The listener should try to understand the *reason* for the feelings rather than being judgmental about them.

**Non-Verbal Messages:** The skillful listener perceives not only the verbal but also non-verbal messages. Every communication situation includes non-verbal cues. The non-verbal messages are more ambiguous than verbal. Because listeners are not careful when interpreting non-verbal cues, it is easy to make faulty generalizations and stereotype people. Non-verbal messages include tone of voice, the expression of face and hands, body posture, and timing of response.

**Listening to others summary:** While we tend to know most of these things, we often forget or even fail to bring them to our conscious mind when we are supposedly listening. Being mindful is most important.

**Listening to Yourself:** *8 Dimensions of Wellness*

**Background:** As we work to improve how we listen to others, we also need to consider how we listen to ourselves, particularly in the area of wellness. Here at OSU, students are our focus. In one of the undergraduate classes I teach, we challenge them to consider their personal *wellness* across various dimensions.

Below, I have extracted eight areas for consideration. These ideas apply to students and adults. Please consider each dimension and its definition. Then, jot a few ideas in the boxes to the right answering the prompt question.

| Listening to Yourself: *8 Dimensions of Wellness* | |
|---|---|
| **Categories:** | *How are you doing in this dimension right now?* (Listen to your internal voice. What is it saying to you?) |
| **Career** – You gain personal satisfaction in your work consistent with your values, goals and lifestyle. | |
| **Digital** – You consider the impact of your virtual presence and use of technology on your overall well-being. | |
| **Emotional** – You can identify, express, and manage the entire range of feelings (e.g., coping with stress). | |
| **Financial** – You know your financial state. You budget, save, and manage finances to achieve realistic goals | |
| **Intellectual** – You value lifelong learning and seek to foster critical thinking. | |
| **Physical** – The physically well person gets adequate sleep, eats a nutritious diet, engages in exercise. | |
| **Social** – You have a network of support based on interdependence, mutual trust, respect. | |
| **Spiritual** – You seek harmony and balance by openly exploring the depth of human purpose. | |

**Internal Listening Challenge:** Look at your responses above. Consider how you are doing in each dimension. Now answer this: ***What advice would you give a friend who had questions about any given area? What could you tell them to help?*** NOTE: Your advice is likely applicable in your own life.

**Follow-up:** Ask your mentee how they feel about their ability to listen well, to others and to themselves. Discuss possible approaches they might use for improvement. Challenge them to consider how they listen to themselves.

## For additional reference / reading:

*Dimension* elements based on OSU Student Wellness Center materials and other research studies. *Listening to Others* based on various Extension mentoring resources by Ken Lafontaine and others (circa 1990s).

# Conversations with Questions for Career Advancement

 **Conversation #15**

### Who You Are vs. What You Do

**Question Preview:** *Who do you want to become?*

**Purpose:** To help your mentee think about who they are or who they want to become instead of the classic question which asks what they want *to do*. This applies to you, the mentor as well.

**Background:** What is the one thing people almost always asked you when you were young? For many, we heard the repeated question, *"What do you want to be when you grow up?"* Some of us imagined firefighting, others considered becoming a nurse, doctor, or teacher. I doubt any of us said, *"Unemployed,"* (although more than a few of us likely imagined a life of leisure).

Asking *"Who do you want to become?"* is qualitatively different from the normal inquiries we get as children about *what* we want to be. Although it is fine to prompt children to think about the future and a possible profession, most children are unequipped to respond thoughtfully.

When we ask the *what* question of teens, we frequently either suppose they have had some guidance in thinking (e.g., a high school career assessment instrument), or we assume they have at least considered some options for future work. These may both be mistakes. Many students have not taken an assessment, and many have never been encouraged to really think through what they enjoy doing, what they are good at (natural gifts), and where they want to learn more. When coupled with what is needed (in business, society, the home, etc.), this is the trifecta that can point to future career satisfaction.

**The Discussion:** First, ask your mentee to think about the main question adults seem to always ask children about their future. Let your mentee respond. If needed, prompt them: *We ask children what they want to be when they grow up. Right?*

Then, mention to your mentee that you want to ask them a qualitatively different question—one that has a metacognition component that might engage their brain in a unique way. This is, perhaps, a question that few, if any, have asked them.

**Who do you want to become?**

Let the question hang there. Watch for their reaction. Many people have never been asked this. It is the opposite of what we've been trained to expect. (i.e., What is your next career move? What position are you hoping to attain?) The question may take a moment to sink in.

**Summary:** Give your mentee some grace. Smile. Assure them that they do not need to answer this question right then, on the spot. Challenge them to ponder it over the coming days and weeks. Challenge them to jot down some thoughts. Then circle back at your next meeting.

**Challenge question:** Ask the person you're mentoring this one final question. It can help them think about how to achieve the *who* they want to become.

**What are some things you could begin doing to get there (to become the person you want to be)?**

**Follow-up:** Ask the person you're mentoring how they felt about this conversation. Challenge them to do the *Personal Mission* and *5 Things* exercises found in this book. These can be of great help.

## Conversation #16

### What's Motivating Your Mentee?

**Question Preview:** *What's motivating you? (Seriously. What's motivating you to get out of bed in the morning? ...to go to work and do a good job? ...to exercise, or not exercise? ...to make someone proud of you?)*

**Purpose:** To understand the basic premise and to consider how you might approach the topic of motivation with your mentee.

**Background & Discussion:** Begin by asking your mentee a simple question:

 **What motivates you?**

Allow them time to reflect and respond. Then, share some findings from studies on motivation:

At the most basic level, most humans are driven by two forms of motivation: **intrinsic** and **extrinsic**. Leadership development consultant at the OSU Fisher College of Business, Dr. Meng Li suggests, *"true and enduring motivation only comes from within."*

Extrinsic motivators come from the outside and include things like money, power and prestige, where you work, and the quality of management. Here, people pursue the goal simply because of the visible, external reward or punishment. Intrinsic motivators come from within. With intrinsic motivators, people pursue the goal because they enjoy the work and find some kind of inherent satisfaction that feeds their life purpose or mission.

> *"People are always motivated. The question is not if they are motivated, but why they are motivated."* – Susan Fowler

Author Susan Fowler outlines four components that **intrinsic motivation** has in the workplace:

- **Competence:** you have the necessary skills to perform work / activities
- **Meaning:** your work goal or purpose aligns with your personal ideals or standards
- **Autonomy:** you have some level of control over your choices or behaviors
- **Impact:** you can influence the strategy, administration, or outcomes

After sharing these four points, ask your mentee:

 **How might you activate these intrinsic motivators, especially if you're feeling bored or stuck?**

Here are two strategies that might help.

1. Find ways to make tasks more interesting. Ask your supervisor if you could try different projects to add variety to your work.
2. Think about how your work has meaning. How can it have a substantial impact on the lives and work of other people? Really push them on this one. Have them make a mental link between

their specific job tasks and their organization's mission. This is powerful.

Ask your mentee if they think these approaches might help. Then share this story:

### A Motivation Story from Steve Jobs:

How did a young tech company start-up CEO motivate the president of Pepsi to quit and come to work for him? He asked a poignant question: *"Do you want to sell sugar water for the rest of your life, or do you want to come with me and change the world?"* The CEO was Steve Jobs, and he lured a highly successful John Scully away from a high-level position by triggering an intrinsic motivation. Both leaders recognized that their **why** was more important than their **what**. For Scully, Pepsi was a job, not his mission. It was a *what*, not his *why*. Jobs help him differentiate the two.

**Follow-up:** Ask your mentee how they felt about the conversation. For this specific topic, ask them to jot down a few items over the next week or so that come to mind about their motivations. Label it "My Motivation List" or something similar. Bring that list next time. Also, challenge them to tell you about how their job tasks link to their organization's mission.

### My Motivation List:

-

-

-

## Sources and Additional Reading:

Batts, Richard (2021). Why Motivating People Doesn't Work and What Does. Published Oct. 25, 2012 at: https://fisher.osu.edu/blogs/leadreadtoday/why-motivating-people-doesnt-work-and-what-does

Fowler, Susan (2017). Why Motivating People Doesn't Work and What Does: The New Science of Leading, Energizing and Engaging. Berrett-Koehler Publishers.

Li, Meng (2018). The Science of Motivation. Published October 10, 2018 at: https://fisher.osu.edu/blogs/leadreadtoday/blog/the-science-of-motivation

Rana, Zat (2017). Career strategy: Don't sell sugar water. Published Fri, Mar 24 2017 at: https://www.cnbc.com/2017/03/24/career-strategy-dont-sell-sugar-water.html

 ## Conversation #17

### Change. Growth Mindset. Ambiguity.
### 3 Skills for Career Advancement

**Question Preview:** *Can you demonstrate how you handle change, have a growth mindset, and deal with ambiguity? (If so, advancement in your career will become accelerated.)*

**Purpose:** To help your mentee consider three critical skills that, if communicated and demonstrated, will absolutely help them capture the attention of their supervisor (or a hiring manager) and help propel their career advancement.

**Background:** Gary Burnison, Korn Ferry CEO and leadership guru (my designation), recently posted that he believes (having seen it in his lived experience) if a person can learn to demonstrate three critical professional skills, they can more quickly advance in their career. In short, he argues they must understand how they: 1. Handle change, 2. Have a growth mindset, and 3. Deal with ambiguity.

I believe we all would benefit from considering these points.

**Discussion:** Ask your mentee this straightforward, but deep question:

 **What do you want to be known for?**

Let them ponder that for a few moments. Then share what Burnison says about how we can begin this journey by understanding how we're wired. This starts with self-reflection. As humans, we sometimes (or often?) overestimate our strengths and underestimate our blind spots. But if we can bring in an outside perspective such as a coach or mentor, we can more accurately see ourselves and better understand our abilities, passion, and purpose, alongside our motivators.

During your discussion, explain these three keys that can help someone stand out in an organization:

1. **Change:** Oprah Winfrey said, *"The greatest discovery of all time is that a person can change his future by merely changing his attitude."* So when change hits our workplaces (or lives), is our attitude one of immediate resistance? Or do we **engage our curiosity and wonder**? e.g., *"Could this result in something good?"*
2. **Growth Mindset:** Carol Dweck's research suggests people with a growth mindset believe that, even if they struggle with certain skills, their abilities are not set in stone. They understand that with work, their skill sets can improve over time.
3. **Ambiguity:** This one is more difficult because, by definition, it's inexact! Burnison defines dealing with ambiguity as knowing how to *"make good decisions based on limited knowledge, or the information you have at the time."* This takes some guts. Deciding and acting without knowing the whole picture can be frightening,

especially when budgets or jobs are on the line. But one can learn to gather information from diverse sources, weigh the data, and ultimately mitigate the risk and uncertainty.

Then, ask your mentee to jot down some ideas around these three questions:

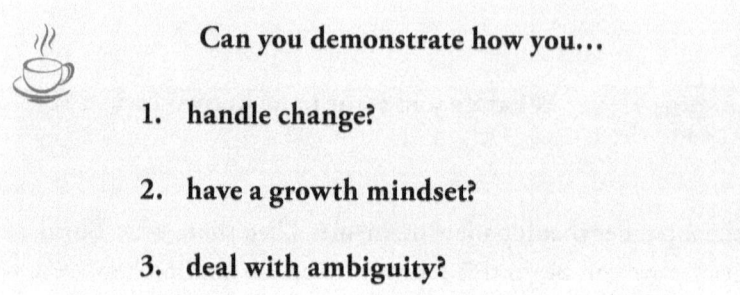

**Can you demonstrate how you…**

1. handle change?
2. have a growth mindset?
3. deal with ambiguity?

Give them time to consider each. Ask them to reflect on one or two ideas with you.

**Follow-up:** Ask your mentee how they felt about the conversation. Set the date and time for your next meeting. Ask them to bring any notes they make on these three questions.

## For additional reference / reading:

Burnison, Gary (October 16, 2022). Special Edition. *Our Time to Take Control.*

Dweck, C. S. (2006). Mindset: The new psychology of success. Random House.

**Conversation #18**

## Reframing 6 Stages of a Career (from Ladder to Scaffold)

**Question Preview**: *Do you have a career path in mind?* Have you heard about climbing the proverbial corporate ladder? Would having a plan or vision of your future help you create a positive and contributory career path?

**Purpose:** To gain an understanding of six elements that can direct a self-fulfilling career path.

**Background & Discussion:** When I was in business school (my undergraduate education from Ohio State's Fisher College of Business) in the early 1980s, we often talked about and likely imagined climbing the proverbial corporate ladder. That was the vision we had of our future; however, few of us really understood what it meant. It wasn't until I was working in a Fortune 500 in the late 1980s that I began to see the reality of people positioning themselves, jockeying, and sometimes yes, stepping on other's fingers as they climbed each rung of that ladder. Was it worth it? Did attaining that next promotion lead to fulfillment?

You can easily find quotes from successful people including athletes, actors, and corporate giants who have said something like this:

> *"I spent all this time climbing to the top; but when I got there, it felt meaningless, and I discovered I was all alone."*

So what might be an alternate ending? Here are some questions to consider:

>  **Reframing Questions:**
>
> 1. What if you invest in career growth while also encouraging and helping others along the way?
>
> 2. What if you imagine your career as a scaffold that provides amazingly strong support and, unlike a ladder, allows more than one person on the platform at a time?

Though he does not use my scaffolding metaphor, Korn Ferry CEO Gary Burnison outlines six phases of a career that offer growth and opportunity at each level. I have used his headings but offer my insights.

Six Stages of Career Growth in brief:

1. **Follower:** These are usually the early years, a first (or even second) job, often just out of college. Burnison notes here, *"You will never lead if you don't know how to follow someone!"*
2. **Collaborator:** As you establish and demonstrate your strengths (check out Gallup's "Strength Finder"), you will begin contributing to both small and large teams. Burnison notes you are still *"operating from your technical skill set,"* but this process will allow you to develop critical skills with people and teams.
3. **Instructor:** While still early in your career, you will find opportunities to lead and subsequently offer instructions to others (individually or on a team). Here, try to operate from both your technical and people skill sets. Use outside collaborators and experts so you can learn and grow even as the instructor. It's true that the earnest teacher learns more than the student.
4. **Manager:** Now, you are beginning to officially manage people. (What?! Don't you manage things and lead people?!) Sure. But you also manage people. This will include adding skills on motivation and mission. You may be setting goals and objectives or providing

strategy. Review Simon Sinek's *Start with Why*. Encourage folks to think about mission every day.

5. **Influencer:** This is not the social media flash in the pan. This is a legitimate platform on which you can begin leveraging your technical and people skills for positive impact. Burnison says influence is a key leadership skill that is needed, particularly in distributed systems where everyone is not in your building. Today's workforce is often remote. Gaining skills to connect with them first will enhance your ability to influence.

6. **Leader:** This level may arise sooner than you expect. And not everyone is ready for it. Here, your time is invested in empowering and inspiring others. Burnison posits the idea that ***the leader is no longer telling people what to do, but is providing guidance on what to think about, and motivating them to reach their potential.*** (Please read that last sentence twice.)

After reviewing these with your mentee, ask them:

1. **Do you have a career path in mind?**

2. **Do you wish to climb the proverbial corporate ladder?**

3. **Would having a plan or vision of your future help you create a positive and contributory career path?**

Allow them some reflection time. Ask them to comment on a few of the thoughts that come to mind.

**Summary:** Studies have shown that compensation and work-life balance are highly desired by today's workers. Opportunities for career growth and influence often rank as high, particularly with today's emerging workforce.

**Metacognitive Minder:** Perhaps this approach can help those we mentor think about scaffolding their career and provide a vision of a path that not only helps them advance, but also demonstrates how they can help others along the way.

*Platforms on scaffolding are large enough for several people.*

As you provide mentoring on career advancement, encourage your protégé to 1.) assess where they are now; 2.) investigate options for advancement; 3.) prepare by taking classes or completing training or shadow exercises; 4.) be ready to shift when opportunity arises.

## For additional reference / reading:

Burnison, G. (no date). 6 Stages of Career Growth: Where are you? Korn Ferry. https://www.kornferry.com/insights/this-week-in-leadership/six-stages-of-career-growth

 ## Conversation #19

### Handling Critics and Criticism: A Growth Mindset Approach

**Question Preview:** *How can you handle and leverage input from critiques and critics?*

**Purpose:** To help your mentee build resilience and leverage critiques and criticism for good.

**Background:** Have you ever felt the gut-punch of a poor annual evaluation? Or have you had so much red ink on a paper it was hard to see what you originally wrote? (Look back at my Conversation #8 in which I describe how I begin each of my graduate courses by sharing my past feedback:

"This paper has too many flaws to be revised." "This [paper] would benefit from getting help from someone who is experienced in writing...")

But I quickly follow up by sharing *the rest of the story*. This is not past feedback I've given students, but criticism I've received! Then I emphasize one thing: *I want your writing to improve here, in the safety of this class, so you will never feel the gut-punch of this kind of criticism in real life.*

Each semester since I began teaching, my SEIs (student evaluation of instruction) have consistently hit the highest levels. I don't think that's because I'm such a great, brilliant professor. (I'm laughing as I write this!) Instead, I believe it's because they see that I truly care about them and want them to grow. This is a form of mentoring in the classroom. Let's talk about how you can help someone you are mentoring leverage input (feedback / criticism) from critiques and critics without giving up or feeling beaten up.

Here's the question for your mentee (with some ideas that follow):

 **How can you handle and leverage input from critiques and critics?**

**The Discussion:** While sometimes (often) difficult to hear or read, critiques and even outright criticism can be leveraged to help us improve. There is, however, one critical step successful folks take that makes it work:

*Force your brain to hear the feedback being as directed to your work, NOT toward yourself.*

Yes, there are critics who throw darts at the person, but *meaningful* evaluation or feedback is aimed at the work. Here's a two-step process outlining how to receive this kind of input:

1. Remove yourself from the equation. Even if the criticism appears (or is) aimed directly at you,

a. Change the words in your head from, *"I'm no good at this"* to *"This is something I still need to learn."* Or, *"Maybe these ideas will help."*
b. Change the words in your head from, *"They're criticizing ME!"* to *"This is a critique aimed at helping improve this work."*

2. Then, dispassionately use the input to find areas for improvement. Once you're past the, *"You need to start over,"* you can look at each suggestion (critique), evaluate how it might help, and then begin making changes for improvement.

**A Challenge for Your Mentee:** *Adopt a Growth Mindset*

Again, critique and criticism can easily make a person *feel* as if they are failing. That's a real thing. But if we can take those thoughts captive and redirect the emotion, we can use the input for improvement. Carol Dweck (2008) has identified a *growth* mindset, as opposed to a *fixed* mindset, as a key to success. She says when people have a fixed mindset, everything is about the outcome. If you fail at something or receive criticism with a fixed mindset, you accept that and give up. If you can adopt a growth mindset, you realize the critiques or criticisms are data that can help you tackle problems, chart a new or redirected course, and continue working for success. This is Dweck's approach. And I must note, it works.

**4 keys to Growth Mindset:**

1. Believe that your *effort* leads to achievements. It's not just inherent talent.
2. Be willing to learn from mistakes. Leverage criticism as input to improve.
3. Know that intelligence and ability can be developed (again, through effort, grit, determination).
4. Embrace asking questions. Ask for help when needed. And admit when you don't know something.

**Summary:** We *will* receive input, feedback, evaluation, and criticism that feels like a gut-punch. Everyone does. But changing the *aim* of the critique (from *me* to *my work*) and adopting a growth mindset can powerfully redirect the situation (and our emotions), leading to improved output.

 **Important Postscript:**

There are critics (and plain old mean people) who may attack you or your work at some time during your life. If or when that happens, ignore everything I wrote above… and then ignore them. Never ever listen to someone who is being mean or attacking you personally. They're not interested in helping. Their critique is not valid. If they're not trying to help, you do not owe them your attention. Every single person has immense value and worth, regardless of our skills (or ability to do some specific task). And as I noted before, every single person knows things we do not. They possess skills we do not. They have gifts we know nothing about. So if someone belittles you, take leave. Go find an encourager who can help you get back on track and make the improvements you want to make. Then, pass it along and encourage someone else.

## For additional reference / reading:

Dweck, C. S. (2008). Mindset: The New Psychology of Success. New York: Ballantine Books.

# Conversation #20

## Providing Clarity

**Question Preview:** *Could honing your ability to provide clarity propel your career advancement?*

**Purpose:** To help your mentee understand how providing clarity to work situations can make them indispensable to their organization.

**Background:** Researchers Jim Kouzes and Barry Posner outlined *5 Practices of Exemplary Leadership* based on years of research with thousands of organizations. Those practices are:

1. Model the Way
2. Inspire a Shared Vision
3. Challenge the Process
4. Enable Others to Act
5. Encourage the Heart

They have also asked people around the globe what they want in a leader. Overwhelmingly, the responses are *honesty, forward-looking, inspiring, and competent*. Three of these are rooted in the construct of credibility. Kouzes and Posner say *personal credibility* is the foundation of leadership.

Leadership guru Andy Stanley cites "integrity" as a number one leadership characteristic people want. Though nuanced, *credibility* and *integrity* are quite similar to the point that they could be labeled synonyms.

In mentoring, one objective is to help our protégé grow into leadership roles. So sharing Kouzes and Posner's research is a great first step. Stanley's books and podcasts are extraordinary as well. In our mentoring, we have an opportunity to share a critical point from Stanley on leadership that could be a game-changer.

**The Discussion:** Stanley says people don't actually follow people because of their integrity. We do indeed *value* integrity, *but we follow clarity*. We follow the person who can outline a simple, clear path forward. He notes, *"Clarity results in **influence** which is the essence of leadership."* He contends clarity is magnetic. Clarity is about the future.

> **Key point:** If someone can be clear (or provide clarity) especially in problem identification, planning, or vision casting, they will be followed.
>
> **To do:** Coach your mentee on looking for opportunities to bring clarity to confusion. Help them hone the skill. Note opportunities such as providing clarity at the end of a meeting or a conversation, regardless of where they are or how long they have been there.
>
> Ask them the question below. Then listen for their responses or any ah-ha ideas.
>
>  **Could honing your ability to provide clarity propel your career advancement?**

**Summary:** Work with your mentee on the idea of clarity. Challenge them to find opportunities and to let you know how it goes. (i.e., Ask them to text or email you if they try this out at work.)

## Additional reading:

Kouzes, J.M. & Posner, B.Z. (2012). The Leadership Challenge (5$^{th}$ ed.). John Wiley & Sons.

Stanley, Andy (2016). *Making Vision Stick*. Leadercast 2016: Architects of Tomorrow. Available at: https://youtu.be/zAOg_rGVlr4

**Conversation #21**

## Triangulating Your Skills, Abilities, and Interests to Find Your Future

**Question Preview:** *What three things could you bring together that will propel you toward the future career and life you desire?*

**Purpose:** To help your mentee think through three items: 1.) what they enjoy doing, 2.) what they are good at (i.e., natural gifts), and 3.) where do they want to learn more. Bringing these three together can powerfully steer someone toward their desired future.

**The Discussion:** Most people have multiple gifts. Many people have the ability to do a variety of jobs, and career paths are frequently not linear. Anecdotally, my friends and former students share that their journeys have been directed more by chance than any kind of plan. That's okay if you are lucky. But many folks find themselves in ho-hum jobs they could take or leave.

So how can you change this approach?

I mentioned in Conversation #12 that we often prompt children to think about their future and possible professions by asking that age-old question: *"What do you want to do when you grow up?"* But even if they have taken some high school career assessments, the Myers-Briggs, or other employment interest instrument, many younger people have never thought through what they enjoy doing, what they are good at (natural gifts), and where they want to learn more. As I noted before, when coupled with what is needed (in business, society, the home, etc.), this is the trifecta that can point to future career satisfaction.

**The Process:** Ask your mentee to consider these questions (while you are meeting with them). Have them jot down a few ideas under each. Listen closely to their responses. Then encourage them to take their list and consider it over the next few weeks.

When answering these questions, do so in the context of considering your future career or *potential* employment:

1. **What do you enjoy doing?**

2. **What are you good at (natural gifts)?**

3. **What do you want to learn more about?**

Ask your mentee this final challenge question:

**Imagine bringing those three things together. What field or job might you aim for in the future?**

**Summary:** This simple exercise can help your mentee begin directing their career path while simultaneously aligning it with their personal interests and life goals.

**Follow-up:** Ask your mentee to share any additional thinking, ah-ha ideas, or direction at your next meeting.

## Conversation #22

### The Resume & Cover Letter (Helping your mentee achieve their next position)

**Question Preview:** *Can your resume get past the first and second round AI (artificial intelligence) screening? Does your cover letter include keywords from the position description?*

**Purpose:** To help your mentee understand AI and applicant tracking systems (ATS) that recruiters and employers use to collect and sort job applications and to provide some tips when applying.

**Background:** There is a lot of advice out there on designing resumes and cover letters. My advice on clarity (a conversation in this book) is a key starting point. In short, be clear. Be succinct. Help your organization sort through the noise.

The main thing today's applicants need to understand is that they must get past the AI (artificial intelligence) that is doing the initial (and sometimes secondary) screening for almost every job. Applicant tracking systems (ATS) have been in wide use for quite a while and are becoming more sophisticated. Your objective is to have the right mix of keywords without going overboard so a real person will give your resume a look.

**The Discussion:** Ask your mentee if they realize or understand how AI screening works.

> **Can your resume get past first and second round AI (artificial intelligence) screening?**
> **Does your cover letter include keywords from the position description?**

Then share these tips that might help.

1. **Do not use columns** in your resume. It may or may not confuse AI or screen readers. The jury is out; but most websites advise against columns. So play it safe.

2. **Capture attention.** Write yourself a tag line. I have worked with over 100 organizations on rethinking their mission statement (which, often, is unknown to the majority of their team). The main issue is that it's too long and complex. Your resume is like that too. You want to include all the pertinent details. At the top, you *need* to capture the eight seconds of attention you're afforded

when a human eye actually reviews your document. Give them your *tag line*. Pull them in.

3. **Be judicious** in your attempt to game the system. Yes, you should work to match keywords in the position description with keywords in your resume. But don't go overboard with this. The new AI can recognize those attempting to sneak in.

   Here's an example that worked:

   *In 2019, my nephew wrote a short computer program that would help him get past the early AI that was being deployed to vet candidates in his field of engineering. His approach was to match keywords (which is now ubiquitous, of course), and get an actual person to see his resume. It worked. He quickly became employed and is now working for a known upstart helping to plan a mission to Mars. (Yes. Literally.)*

   *The key point is this: Match keywords from the position description. But do not go overboard.*

4. **Return to the fundamentals.** By this, I mean write your resume to tell your story. After you get past the AI, a real person will recognize a person who has real-life experience… AND who has reflected on it to understand what they have learned and how they can apply that in their next position.

   Here's an example from my work:

   *I have worked with numerous undergraduate students here at Ohio State who will list some type of restaurant work on their resume. That's good. But instead of simply stating the position, I advise them to write about what they learned. If one wants to stand out, they must describe the higher level (metacognition) of the work.*

*For example:* Instead of listing "server at X restaurant"... rephrase, "Used my emotional intelligence skills to recognize customer needs and respond appropriately to create a positive experience which at times included creative thinking and problem identification."

**Summary:** Know that AI will be screening your resume. Create one that will advance you to the next step so your real self and ability can shine.

## Conversation #23

### Real Interview Tips that Work

**Question Preview:** *What is the most important thing to consider when preparing for an interview?*

**Purpose:** This conversation will help the person you are mentoring think about key points in preparing for a potential career-changing interview.

**Background:** Throughout my career, I have interviewed hundreds of people for positions ranging from entry-level laborers (in my industrial manufacturing days) to executives (including corporate, non-profit, and higher education leaders with earned doctorates). I've done one-on-one and team interviews. I've done formal and informal. I've met people well-prepared, and those who may not have even known why they were there. Over these 35+ years, I've observed several key points worth sharing.

As I noted in the *Resume and Cover Letter* conversation, there is a lot of good advice out there on interviewing. So of course, encourage your mentee to read through tips on LinkedIn, Handshake, and other job boards. But then challenge them:

>  **What is the most important thing to consider when preparing for an interview?**

This is a tricky question because, arguably, there is no correct answer. Please read on. I outline some basics and contend that there is *one major opportunity* that is sometimes missed.

**Preparation to Ensure Success:**

The purpose of an interview is to showcase your skills, experience, and personality to a hiring manager or team in a short amount of time. That window may be in person, or online. This is the final step before landing your dream job, but interviewing can be a stressful experience. That stress can be reduced by some simple preparation. Here are the basics:

1. **Research the company:** Before your interview, learn all about the company and the job. Know their mission, history, products, and services. Take note of any recent news articles. The best candidates I have ever interviewed were those who related their personal mission to our corporate mission.
2. **Practice your responses:** There are lists of common interview questions that should be familiar to you. Practice responding with a friend or family member. Practicing will help you feel more comfortable during the actual interview and ensure that you are able to articulate your skills and experience in a clear and concise manner.
3. **Dress appropriately:** Whether in person or online, dress professionally. Our society judges people on *first impressions*. Make yours count. If your interview is online, stand up if able. Standing is a bold statement that you are ready to run. Also, position your camera to frame a positive background or scene.
4. **Be on time:** Arrive on time or log in early. This punctuality shows your respect for the interviewer's time.
5. **Listen:** Instead of formulating responses in your mind, listen carefully to the interviewer's questions. Feel free to pause, reflect,

and then provide examples of YOUR experience. It's also okay to ask them to repeat or restate a question.
6. **Follow up:** After the interview, send a thank you email or note to the interviewer. This will show you appreciate their time and are interested in the position.

Again, these six tips are generic, but there is the one key thing that is sometimes missed:

> *During the interview, you must convey how your education, training, experience, and personal mission link with their corporate mission.* Say aloud: *"I want my work to help move us toward the mission of x, y, z." (Fill in with their mission brief.)*

This is what will land you the job.

**Summary:** Ask your mentee to share a copy of their resume. Look it over. Provide some feedback.

 **Conversation #24**

### The Stay Interview: Is Staying an Opportunity?

**Question Preview:** *Are you thinking of staying or leaving your current employer?* Could one of those be a positive career strategy? Which would propel your career more quickly?

**Purpose:** To help your mentee gain a larger vision of why and how staying can be a positive contribution to their employer and can help advance their career. These questions can also be considered to determine if changing jobs might be beneficial.

**Background:** Employee turnover rates have increased dramatically in recent years. Blame it on COVID, the gig economy, pay/benefit differentials, metal health stressors, generational change, or life balance, but turnover is real. It has direct costs in time (hiring process, onboarding, new person becoming effective) and dollars (customer/order loss, unemployment costs, etc.). There's also an institutional knowledge or team contributor loss that can derail new or ongoing work.

With so much change, could the person you are mentoring benefit by staying with their organization? Could staying be a career advancement strategy?

Most organizations use Richard Finnegan's seminal idea of the stay interview to learn what actions can improve employee engagement and retention. In mentoring, I believe you can modify the idea and conduct a brief, non-formal conversation with your mentee to help them gain insight around their current position and consider opportunities that might avail themselves by staying there or leaving. Investing time in thinking this through is key.

**The Discussion:** Here are four essential questions you can use to conduct a non-formal stay interview:

1. Are you thinking of staying or leaving your current employer?
2. Could one of these be a positive career strategy?
3. Or would changing jobs propel you more quickly?
4. As organizations see increased turnover, what opportunities may exist if you stay?

**The Stay Interview:** Ask your mentee to consider these questions *to help them determine potential career movements.*

1. What do you look forward to when you come to work each day?
2. What do you like least about working here?
3. What keeps you working here?
4. What might tempt you to leave?
5. If you could change something about your job, what would that be?
6. What talents are not being used in your current role?
7. Are there other positions at your current organization that you could aim for advancement?

**For additional reference / reading:**

Finnegan, Richard (2015). The Stay Interview. Finnegan Institute. AMACOM Books. Additional information: https://www.finneganinstitute.com/stay-interviews/

SHRM (Society for Human Resource Management) (n.d.) Stay Interview Questions. Available at: https://www.shrm.org/resourcesandtools/tools-and-samples/hr-forms/pages/stayinterviewquestions.aspx

## Conversation #25

### Financial Health: 2 Keys for Success Today and in Retirement (Live and Give)

**Question Preview:** *Do you want financial freedom now and when you retire?*

**Purpose:** To suggest two critical (yet doable) actions that can put you on track for financial stability while you are working and set you up to retire the way you want.

**Background:** When I was in my early twenties, an "old" guy at work (he was probably forty or forty-five!) took me to lunch one day and asked me about my financial plan for the future. He said it was time for me to begin long-term retirement savings. Dave Uhrig's advice started me on a path for financial success. Thirty years later, I discovered Dave Ramsey (with his highly effective debt-snowball / everyday-millionaire approach) and realized how lucky I was to have had the early advice from my slightly older and wiser work colleague.

Over the past twenty-plus years, I have taken time to share this advice from both Daves with younger colleagues at work, when volunteering, or even talking with many of my seventeen nieces and nephews. A few have called to thank me and share how they never realized how much their long-term savings (the nest egg) would mean to them. Their appreciation is palpable. There's no better feeling than knowing you helped someone gain financial freedom.

And guess what? You can do it too. You can do it today. There's no need to take a class or study the stock market. You can coach your mentee (or anyone) on personal finance using simple, proven advice.

**The Discussion:** There are two things almost anyone can do that will enhance future financial security and success. These ideas work at almost any salary level. [Though I must note that there are folks today who are not paid a living wage. Here, we must be mindful of that situation, and advocate for improvements while still working to help them formulate a budget or plan for spending.]

Here's how it works. First, encourage your mentee to think about their finances and future. Many people procrastinate planning or saving. Stop the procrastination. Sit down and draw up a plan. It need include only two items:

>  **A plan for financial freedom:**
>
> **Are you willing to:**
>
> 1. Live (on less than you make)
> 2. Give (to causes or needs of others)

*Living and retiring well is not about math.* It's psychology. It's about our philosophical constructs on *how* we think about money. It's about discipline. We must learn to *live* below our financial means and *give* as an act of understanding that we can survive and even thrive on, for example, 90% of our income. There's also intrinsic joy that comes from acting in a selfless manner, which further enhances living.

Here are the details. When you live on less than you make, you are automatically set up to survive a lower retirement income. For example, experts often mention needing 70-80% of your pre-retirement income to live "comfortably" in retirement. (e.g. $50,000 final working salary = needing $35,000 - $40,000 in retirement.) Pro tip: If you live on 80% of your salary today, this problem is greatly eased. That is, you are already saving 10% and giving 10%. So let's talk about how it works.

**Point #1: Live** (but pay attention to the details)

1. Write a spending plan (a.k.a., budget)
2. Reduce eating out (#1 expense for many)
3. Check your subscriptions (cable, streaming services, magazines, music online, and your kids' expenses). These add up wildly.
4. Compare car and home insurance rates. Switch if you can get similar coverage at a better rate.
5. Do an Internet search for: "Biggest non-needed expenses of people" (or something similar).
6. Do a "debt snowball" (pay off your debt from smallest-to-largest). It's a psychological thing.
7. Start a Roth IRA (now).

Ask your mentee these questions about the above seven points:

1. **Which could you begin doing now? Seriously. Today.**

2. **Which could you begin next week?**

3. **Imagine your life in five years: What does it look like if you have followed these concepts? How might you feel inside?**

Time is your friend. Last year, I planted a tree in our backyard as shade for our deck. It will take some time (many years) for it to really help. I've been kicking myself because I should have done it twelve years ago when we first moved in! *It's the same with retirement savings.* Time is of the essence.

How much will you need in retirement? These questions will help you plan:

1. If you have a house/land, will it be paid off?
2. What are the ongoing taxes, insurance, and upkeep each year?
3. If you plan to rent, what's your ongoing monthly cost (with inflation)?
4. Are you the "new car" type?
5. Do you want to help kids/grandkids pay for college?
6. Do you want to travel the world?
7. Do you want to do volunteer work?
8. Do you want to work part time?

Ask your mentee these questions about the above eight points:

1. Which is most important?
2. Which is not necessary, but perhaps a desired option?
3. Imagine your life in your retirement years: What does it look like if you have followed these concepts? How might you feel inside?

**Point #2: Give** (to causes or needs of others). This changes your thinking. When you freely give money away (with no strings attached) several things happen:

- You help others (a cause, a person, etc.).
- You focus on others and become less self-centric (which research shows is a positive path for joy and satisfaction in life).
- You learn self-discipline. (Again, read the research on the benefits of this.)
- You train your brain to recognize and remember your good fortune (e.g., of having a job). This increases internal gratitude and improves health according to research studies.

Talk with your mentee on this topic of how to achieve giving freedom. Have them look at the four items above and ask:

1. Which sounds most important to you? Why?
2. If you could learn more about one of the items, which would it be? How might that help you?

Here are some final additional challenge questions:

>  **Additional questions for financial freedom:**
>
> Do you want financial freedom now and when you retire?
>
> Are you willing to consider these two ideas: to live and to give?
>
> Imagine your life in 5 years: What does it look like if you have followed these concepts? How might you feel inside?

**Additional Discussion on the Historic Roots of Giving:** (if time permits)

There is a tremendous amount of ancient wisdom on giving. In Judaism (the Mosaic Law), they stipulated a "tithe" which literally meant giving 10% of your wealth. In Christianity, Jesus extended the meaning of a tithe to make it less legalistic and more heartfelt. In Islam, the Zakat ("alms giving") is one of the Five Pillars. In Sikhism, they encourage the Dasvandh (giving one tenth). And outside of religious tenets, non-religious and secular writings have wonderful ideas of *Giving What We Can* (GWWC) for altruistic associations in which members pledge at least 10% of their income to charities.

Apart from the ancient wisdom on giving, today Warren Buffet has set the example of donating 99% of his wealth to charity. He says, *"Possessions end up possessing the owner. The asset I most value are interesting, diverse, and long-standing friends."* In a research study, Elizabeth Dunn (2014) at the University of British Columbia and Harvard Business School found that people who spent as little as $5 on someone else were happier compared with people who were asked to spend $5 on themselves. Numerous other studies on the benefits of giving show increased happiness and fulfillment.

Finally, in the *Book of Joy*, His Holiness the Dalai Lama and Archbishop Desmond Tutu (with Doug Abrams) say, *"It seems money can buy happiness, if we spend it on other people."* They cite Davidson & Schuyler (2015) noting generosity is one of the four fundamental brain circuits that map with long-term well-being.

**Summary:** We can train our brains on living and giving. When we tell ourselves we can live on 80% or 90%, we begin to change how we think and feel and act with money. The actions of living and giving can absolutely provide financial peace and security for our future.

**Homework:** Make a retirement Bucket List. Whether you're 20 or 40 or 60. Make a list of what you want to retire to. (i.e., Don't retire *from* something; but retire *to* something new.) Then ponder how adopting *living and giving* now can make it happen.

## For additional reference / reading:

Ramsey, Dave. (2007). *The Total Money Makeover: A Proven Plan for Financial Fitness.* Nelson Books.

# Conversations with Questions for Expanding Points of View

 **Conversation #26**

### E+R=O (Event + Response = Outcome)

**Question Preview:** *How do you change a gut reaction to a thoughtful response in the moment?*

**Purpose:** To help your mentee (and yourself!) improve how you respond to any and all events that occur in day-to-day living.

**The Discussion:** What do you do when someone is tailgating you? And I mean RIGHT UP ON YOUR BUMPER!

We all have options. Right? Do you wave at them (with one finger)? Do you tap the brake pedal? Or do you draw upon your knowledge of the complexities of leadership theory and formulate a proper response in the moment?

> *My alleged tailgating incident:*
>
> *In the summer of 2016, my E+R=O was tested. I remember it as if it were yesterday. Apparently, I was the one driving a bit too close to the person in front of me. (Some, like that driver, might have labeled it tailgating.) Well, when he FINALLY*

*put on his blinker to turn right (and allow me to zoom around him), halfway through the turn, he hit the brakes! I had to swerve to miss rear-ending his car.*

*I couldn't believe it. He brake-checked me. What nerve! At that moment, I really really wanted to wave at him with one finger, but I generally don't do things like that. Instead, I turned my head to glare at him as I went by. And guess what. He was "waving" at me... that one middle finger right up in the air.*

*I was so angry. The nerve. The incredulity.*

*But just as I started to lay on the horn (and really tell him off), I remembered something. My fifteen-year-old daughter was sitting next to me in the passenger seat. We were going to our church parking lot where I could bestow proper driving lessons.*

*At that moment... at that very moment... the formula popped into my head: E+R=O. I'd heard Tim Kight speak several years earlier at a conference where he discussed this exact tailgating scenario. And it hit me right between the eyes.*

What does E+R=O mean?

In 2004, author Jack Canfield outlined this formula to help people improve how they respond to any and all events that occur in day-to-day living. An *event* is anything that happens to you, but especially pronounced when it is an irritation or stressor. His formula is incredibly simple and can help you change a gut reaction to a thoughtful response in the moment. Here is the meaning:

E+R=O (event + response = outcome)

Events happen all day every day. We take great notice of those that are unexpected or stressors. The key is to change your gut reaction to a thoughtful response. In this manner, you are much more likely to achieve the desired outcome. But *how* do you do it?

Kight outlined six steps from a new leadership book (Meyer, 2015) that will help you to achieve this switch from reaction to response. I tried to memorize the list at first, but I quickly discovered one thing: I never even once needed to go beyond item #1: Press pause. Any time any event happens to me, if I can remember to press pause, slow down, and think, it's a game-changer.

After pressing pause, there is one key question to ask yourself:

*What does this situation require of me?*

Here, you are engaging your executive-brain and making a measured response instead of an emotive reaction.

The last key point to remember is this:

*Your Response creates an Event for someone else.*

This is one of the most important points I make in a graduate leadership course I teach. I implore my students to think about this for a minute (or just 15 seconds!). So often, we think our success or failure is determined by what happens (an event) to us. But it's not. It is determined by how we respond.

After discussing the above, ask your mentee:

 **What do you think? How might you respond the next time someone is tailgating you?**

**Follow-up:** Ask your mentee to take five minutes this week and ponder how they might respond the next time someone is tailgating them. Also, ask them to text you when they encounter a stressful "E" but remember the formula. Ask them to share how it felt to change their *reaction* to a *response*.

## For additional reference / reading:

Canfield, Jack (no date). The Success Formula that Puts You in Control of Your Destiny. Available at: https://jackcanfield.com/blog/the-formula-that-puts-you-in-control-of-success/

Canfield, Jack (2004). The Success Principles. New York: Harper Collins.

Kight, Tim (no date). How I learned The E+R=O Mindset and it changed my life. Available at: https://www.tbriankight.com/blog/how-i-learned-the-ero-mindset

Meyer, U., & Coffey, W. R. (2015). Above the line: Lessons in leadership and life from a championship season. New York: Penguin Press.

 **Conversation #27**

### Circle of Control: Shift Your Focus; Reduce Worry

**Question Preview:** *Why do we worry about things we cannot control? How could we shift our focus to become more productive and less anxious?*

**Purpose:** To help your mentee understand the simple concept of focusing on items within our circles of concern and control.

> **My Challenge:**
>
> *In mid-February 2023, my daughter told me she'd been awarded a full ride to graduate school. I was thrilled! But then she told me it was in Alaska, 3,776 miles away from home. My elation did a one-eighty, and worry immediately*

set in. My mind raced: "I don't know anyone in Alaska." "She'll freeze in Alaska." "Isn't it always dark up there?" The unknown can trigger powerful emotions, especially when it involves someone you love. So what was I to do?

**Background:** In Stephen R. Covey's book, *The 7 Habits of Highly Effective People*, he outlined the idea of a *circle of control* in which we might segregate difficult situations such that we focus our attention on things that matter and that we have some control over. Like the E+R=O formula, this sounds remarkably simple; but it takes time and effort to master.

Covey outlines three levels (circles) for us to consider:

The **Circle of Concern** is outermost. It includes things we often worry about and likely *should* be concerned with but cannot control. Examples include the weather in Alaska, macro politics, gun violence, and the fickle computer in your car flashing dashboard lights at you, seemingly at random.

The **Circle of Influence** includes areas where we can have some choice, action, or impact. In my example, I sought to influence my daughter to *immediately* buy bear spray as soon as the plane landed. I also suggested (more reasonably) she ask her professor if her arrival date could be flexible, allowing her to find a cheaper airline ticket. This would also give her time to learn her way around prior to her research appointment commencing.

The **Circle of Control** is the one we all love. This innermost circle consists of all the things we can take action on. In my challenge above, my very first action was to search the Internet to look at weather, roads, housing, and retail. And guess what? It's not always dark in Alaska! They had a car dealership that could install an engine block heater for those very cold days. I was in my element. I was taking action!

**The Discussion:** We love it when we can control things. We love to take action and make things happen. Here's a question to pose to your mentee about that:

>  **What's the difference between the weather and your mood?**

I love asking people this question. I'm sure you can immediately see where I'm going with it. No one can control whether it rains or snows, or how soon it gets dark (which is only a couple hours a night during summer in Alaska). But we all can decide how it affects us. This is the circle of control.

If we can help those we mentor focus on the things that they can influence or do something about, then they can gain back the time, worry, and anxiety that would have been spent on things they cannot control. Again, concern is legitimate. Conversely, if we can shift our mind to think about what we can influence and control, we can increase our resilience, productivity, and success.

**My Challenge (the results):** After a certain period of worry and anxiety (I won't say how long) about my daughter moving to Alaska, I began to shift my focus to things I might be able to influence or even control. As noted above, I educated myself on life in Alaska, on how to stay safe, and on how my daughter might enjoy the amazing outdoor lifestyle that many embrace being up north.

I still must remind myself (on a regular basis) that I cannot control her aging car's computer (and the dashboard lights that blink at random). We can be *concerned*, and together, we can *control* finding local garages, friendly mechanics, or friends to get a ride when needed.

**Summary:** This framework, the circle of control, can be used by almost anyone at almost any age. Whatever stressor hits you, applying the circles and truly focusing on what you can take action on will help.

**Follow-up:** Ask your mentee how they felt about this conversation. Challenge them to try shifting focus the next time they are worried, and then to tell you about it. Did the circles help?

**Conversation #28**

## Hidden Diversity: A Mentoring Conversation

**Question Preview:** *Can we recognize diversity that is not outwardly visible? Could that diversity have great value to both the mentor and mentee?*

**Purpose:** To help your mentee recognize hidden diversity.

**Background:** If someone saw you and your mentee having coffee, what would they see? Are your skin tones similar or different? Do you share the same gender presentation? How about your socio-economic status: is it revealed in your clothing? What about your ethnicity? Are there any visible cues?

By default, we often initiate mentor relationships based on surface-level data. We know our protégé's name, job title, and how they look outwardly (even if on Zoom). Taking time to dive into the non-visible aspects and experiences of people can deepen your mentoring relationship and serve as a reminder to increase attention each time we meet or interact.

Well here goes. Yes. I am rolling out the old iceberg. I know. I know. My graduate students roll their eyes when this slide shows up. I can hear them whisper with dread, *"He's going to tell us about hidden diversity again."* An occasional soul experiences a sudden need for the rest room.

After acknowledging their pushback, I make one simple statement: *"This is a reminder for me."*

**What people see (above the water line):**

- Outward appearance
- Physical behaviors
- Sound of voice (accents)

**What's hidden (beneath the waves):**

- Values
- Beliefs, worldviews, faith traditions
- Socioeconomic status
- Intelligence, ability
- Mental and physical health
- Pronoun/gender identity, sexual orientations
- Ethnicity
- DNA / physical variation
- History and more

I regularly meet new people, and I talk daily with people I've known for years. But how well do I really know them? How well do they really know me? Aside from a couple of friends in the counselor and clergy professions, I know few who can set aside their first visual impression (or their one-hundredth time seeing someone), truly look beneath the surface, and remind themselves that this person may have sadness or joy of which we know nothing. They may have recently experienced loss or gain, an acute mental health crisis, an ongoing battle with dyslexia, addiction, food insecurity, or any number of other afflictions. We may observe signs, but we simply do not know.

If we do not pause and remind ourselves of these hidden differences, it is easy to interact on the surface in an "I - It" transaction. In *Social Intelligence* (2006), Daniel Goleman describes this as treating others as objects, not persons. The inverse is the "I - You" relationship in which others' feelings not only matter to us but change us. This is a picture of empathy.

So how might discussing *hidden diversity* improve the connection between you and your mentee? Could it help your mentee expand their EQ (emotional intelligence), a skill which Goleman (1995) contends is learnable?

**The Discussion:** Ask your mentee to generate as many ideas as possible on distinct types of hidden diversity.

> ☕ **What are ways people are different that may not be visible on the surface?**
>
> -
>
> -
>
> -

Have them make a list. Then ask which stands out in their mind. Challenge them to look for items they had never considered. Then ask if there is one they might be interested in learning more about with you. Dig deep. Look at the "What's Hidden" list above.

Here is a closing question to ask those you mentor for more personal reflection.

> ☕ **List some aspects of hidden diversity that others may not know about you.**

**Follow-up:** For this conversation, ask your mentee to casually observe someone with whom they interact and wish to know better or improve their relationship. (I would not suggest using this for a romantic goal, although it might help.) Perhaps it's someone on a team at work, or someone they look up to as an informal mentor or sounding board. Ask them to become curious about hidden diversity, and initiate a conversation with that person. At your next meeting, ask how the experience went and whether it helped.

## Conversation #29

### Seek Diverse Relationships

**Question Preview:** *Could we experience more personal and professional growth by increasing the diversity of our relationships?*

**Purpose:** To consider the benefits of having diverse relationships. To open conversations on how all aspects of diversity, equity, and inclusiveness can help.

**The Discussion:** Ask your mentee this simple but critical question:

>  **Do you think having increased diversity in your personal and professional relationships might be helpful?**

Explore their thinking here. Ask if they have many relationships with people who differ from them.

Here are some prompting questions that might help both you and your mentee:

1. How would you relate to or mentor a person 20 years younger than you?
2. What wisdom might you share with someone 10 years older? Could that pairing even work?
3. Would you be comfortable if your friend or mentee had a different skin color?
4. What if you had language barriers?
5. Would you be comfortable with someone who dressed differently (e.g. wore religious-based clothing)?
6. What if they had a different sexual orientation or gender identity?

7. Would you be comfortable working with someone who may be on the autistic spectrum?
8. How might working with someone from a different socio-economic class feel?
9. What if they look the same as you outwardly, but you think or feel you have nothing in common?
10. Is it possible to connect with someone in a meaningful way even though they may be different?

Challenge questions: Have your mentee look at the ten items above. Then ask:

1. **Which two or three stand out in your mind?**

2. **What might you want to learn about the items you listed above?**

3. **How might expanding your diverse relationships benefit you and your work (or volunteer) organization?**

**Metacognition Minder:** Not surprisingly, diverse pairings may produce better results when mentoring. With the additional element of diversity, both the mentor and mentee (or any relationship) can grow, perhaps even more so than in a homogeneous pairing. *Before starting coaching or mentoring work, the key is to* **know yourself***.*

Can you, without thinking too long, describe yourself in a few words? For instance, what are the two words that best describe your philosophy of life? What do you want to be known for? You don't need to use fancy jargon: e.g., *Change agent. Synergy catalyst. Paradigm shifter.* The great -two Heisman Trophy winner Archie Griffin lives by two words: **Attitude and Gratitude.** My two words: **encouragement and gratitude.** I also hold a **personal vision/mission:** *To make a positive impact wherever I go.* It's short and easy to remember.

What are your two words? _____,
_____. What is your mission?

*If you have not thought this through, please see the Personal Mission exercise.* It is likely that you and your mentee (regardless of your differences) can relate to the keywords you each live by. This is a great place to begin diverse conversations.

In *The Light We Carry: Overcoming in Uncertain Times*, Michelle Obama says that each of us "carries a bit of inner brightness, something entirely unique and individual." She reinforces the idea that we must recognize our own light first, and then we can encourage unique qualities in people around us. "Our differences are treasures and they're also tools." But we must be ready to listen. When you are in a mentoring conversation, try to reflect what is being said using their words, not yours. Think about where they are, not where you want them to be. Then, as Michelle notes, the "wholeness of their story" can add to the wholeness of yours. This is how we make meaningful change.

**Summary:** Remember. It starts with you. When reflecting and responding, use two simple statements: *"What I heard you say was…"* and, *"Tell me more about what you meant when you said…"*

**Follow-up:** Ask your mentee how they felt about the conversation. Set the date and time for your next meeting.

## For additional reference / reading:

Obama, M. (2022). The Light We Carry: Overcoming in Uncertain Times. Crown Publishing.

**Conversation #30**

## Building Your Emotional Intelligence (EQ)

**Question Preview:** *What's your EQ? Can you grow and develop it?*

**Purpose:** To help your mentee understand and grow their EQ.

**Background:** Success in the workplace or classroom parallels success in real life. When I coach leaders or teachers, I often stress the need for strengthening our emotional intelligence *so* we can better relate and improve outcomes. This mirrors work in mentoring.

We often hear people dismissing social / emotional skills as *touchy-feely*. Many still use the term *soft skills*. Over the past dozen years, my interactions with employers (from manufacturing to tech) summarily state that they can teach someone the job, but *"we need people who can communicate and work as a team."* Thus, I summarily dismissed the term *soft skills* years ago. The business, industry, service, and knowledge sectors of our economy are demanding ***critical skills***. These are what we're describing here, and what your mentee needs to understand.

When The Ohio State University's 2020 presidential search committee began their task, one of the desired, critical skills stood out. They listed it in the position: *"Someone with a high EQ."*

So, what is this EQ all about?

**Emotional Intelligence (EI) (EQ)** – This was defined by Daniel Goleman in 1995. I call these other ways *to be smart*. In brief, we must think about:

- how one recognizes their own and other's emotions
- how one discriminates different feelings
- how one uses emotional information to guide thinking and behavior

If you understand your feelings, you may use them to:

- Connect with your students.
- Make better decisions; motivate yourself and others.
- Find empathy; be positive; encourage hope.
- Improve interactions; manage business, professional, student, familial, and personal relationships.

I call the above *meaningful outcomes*. Here's a depiction of the EQ framework:

**An EQ Framework:**

|  | **Self** | **Social** |
|---|---|---|
| **Recognition** (awareness) | Self-Awareness → | Social Awareness |
|  | ↓ | ↓ |
| **Regulation** (management) | Self-Management → | Relationship Management |

**Emotional Intelligence (EQ)** *is based on Personal and Social Competencies:*

1. Self-Awareness – You know your strengths, preferences, resources, intuitions, as well as your limitations. You know your *why* (Sinek, 2009).
2. Self-Regulation – You control and channel events, moods, impulses, and resources.
3. Motivation – You are driven to achieve beyond expectations. *Your emotional tendencies guide or facilitate reaching goals.*
4. Empathy (Social Awareness) – You are aware of feelings, needs, concerns of others. *You thoughtfully consider other's feelings in the process of making intelligent decisions.* [This is highly needed to do teamwork well.]
5. Social Skills – You are adept at managing relationships with others and inducing desirable responses.

**The Discussion:** Share this EQ overview with your mentee. Then have a 30 to 45-minute conversation about the concept. Dig deep. Ask these questions:

>  Do you believe increasing one's EQ can be of benefit? If so, share some ideas.
>
> Which of the 5 EQ competencies might you want to work on? Why?

After hearing their thoughts, challenge them to try increasing their EQ by identifying a self-study book, podcast, or other learning mechanism. And for a final challenge, ask them which areas of self-awareness, self-regulation, motivation, empathy, or social skills they might want to work on. Have them name one or two items.

**Follow-up:** Ask your mentee to identify one of the five competencies Goleman outlines at some point in their upcoming week, and to reflect on that aspect (e.g., when they noticed the need for self-regulation). Discuss this at your next meeting. Encourage them to do some further reading or watch a video/podcast on EQ.

## Conversation #31

### Building Your Social Intelligence

**Key Objectives:** To help your mentees understand and grow their social intelligence.

**Background:** Most of us are familiar with Daniel Goleman's work on emotional intelligence (EQ). About ten years after publishing his seminal work on that subject, he dove even deeper into our brains by examining research on the chemistry and connections that drive us. These, subsequently, allow our societies, workplaces, and families to function and thrive.

In brief, *social intelligence* is a construct that considers our ability to accurately read other people around us, as well as understand the context, and then (the key) act appropriately. That's pretty basic stuff. Goleman goes on to claim that the *way we engage* with our social environment has profound consequences for our external success. Herein, we need to pay attention.

One of the key concepts is to consider how we view ourselves. Goleman notes *"self-absorption in all its forms kills empathy."* If we are focused on self, our world contracts and our problems are all that matter. If we can instead shift our focus to others, our world expands. This mental health benefit has now been measured physiologically. Focusing on others allows our problems to drift to the periphery (and thus seem smaller). This increases our capacity for connection and meaningful action.

**The Discussion:** From a personal and professional development standpoint, Goleman says social intelligence is the sweet spot for achievement. He gives an example that I find highly related to mentoring. Goleman says there are times when we may become *frazzled*, and our emotional upsurges hamper the effective working of our brain's executive center. This immediately *"handicaps our abilities for learning, for holding information, for reacting flexibly, for creativity, for planning and organizing."* These moments can push us into cognitive dysfunction. We are distracted by thoughts that hijack our attention and *"squeeze our cognitive resources."*

Here's a question for your mentee to ponder:

 **How might you cope with (or even prevent) frazzled times?**

Let them ponder this for a moment. Reflect on the *E+R=O* formula. If you remember, there are six things you can do when an *event* occurs. Now, I cannot remember lists very well. But with this formula, I have only ever needed to remember the first item: *Press pause*. Every time I have successfully pressed pause based on an event, I have been able to control my *response* (instead of *reacting*) and achieve a better *outcome*. It works. Social intelligence is a lot about pressing pause.

Challenge your mentee with this final question:

>  **What are some ways increasing your social intelligence might help your personal or professional success?**

**Summary:** Share the idea of social intelligence with your mentee. Then have a 30-minute conversation about the concept. Dig deep. Ask if they believe increasing one's social intelligence can help? Ask how. Challenge them to try it.

## For additional reference / reading:

Goleman, Daniel (2006). Social Intelligence: The New Science of Human Relationships.

# Conversation #32

## Generation C: Mentoring for Connectivity

**Question Preview:** *How can connections help your career and life?*

**Purpose:** To help your mentee consciously think about making connections for success.

**Background:** For years, we have categorized generations of our US population as Boomers, the Gen Xers, the Millennials, and even Gen Z. These distinctions result in both accurate and inaccurate stereotypes. So how do you coach someone who is from a different group, whether they are younger *or* older than you?

Social science tells us we have more in common than differences (think: life goals, joy, struggles, job stress, job success, friendship, family, purpose). Start there. Commonalities connect. The idea of encouraging *connectivity* may be one of the most powerful mentoring suggestions you can make.

**The Discussion:** How do we encourage connectivity? In 2012, digital analyst Brian Solis identified "Generation C" as a group that, regardless of age, was a "Connected Consumer." His definition included anyone who integrates technology into their daily routine. In 2016, Ryan Holmes described the "C" in Gen C as referring to everything from collaboration to community, computerization, and content. He emphasized that the key point was connectivity. In his bestselling book *The Fred Factor*, Mark Sanborn claims it is *humanness* that creates value, and it doesn't have to cost a penny. The person and their ability to *connect* is the resource.

This is nothing new. In the 1980s, we called it "networking." Today, there is the additional, necessary element of using electronic devices to aid and enhance these connections. The idea remains the same. By encouraging the habit of connectivity, those we mentor will see more doors opened and will discover opportunities otherwise missed.

Do you remember the informal definition of "luck"? Some have said it's where preparation meets opportunity. Connectivity can help your mentee create their own luck.

Holmes offers some suggestions for Gen C. He says we should use the breadth of electronic tools now at our disposal not only for passive consumption but for participation. In *Working Out Loud*, John Stepper (2015) describes a way to combine relationships with technology to reach and engage people. He calls it a different approach to networking, and begins by asking three questions:

1. What am I trying to accomplish?
2. Who can help me?

3. How can I contribute to them to deepen our relationship?

Here's the key: Stepper says that instead of connecting to *get something*, we should lead with generosity, *"investing in relationships that give you access to other people, knowledge, and possibilities."* The generosity component is critical. Stepper details three points about the process:

1. Generosity builds relationships, and we are wired for reciprocal altruism.
2. Don't keep score. There's no quid pro quo in play here. You must mean to truly want to help.
3. Be genuine. Do not try to fake your way through this or to construct something that's not you.

Following this approach will allow you or your mentee to benefit as others reciprocate (point #1). Again, you are preparing to meet potential opportunities. Ask your mentee what they think of Stepper's approach. Then ask:

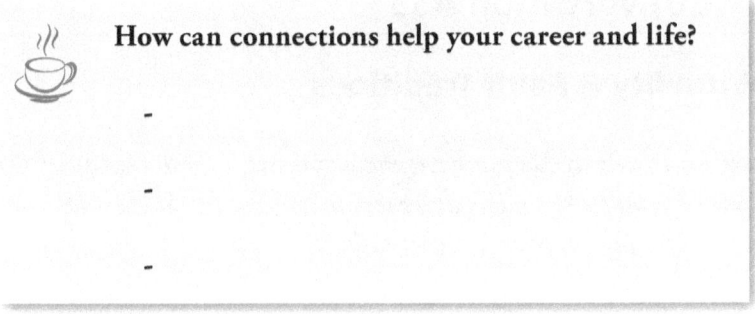

**How can connections help your career and life?**

- 
- 
- 

**Summary:** Don't totally discount the 1980s. Meeting for coffee still works. While you're enjoying the drink, please keep your phone in your pocket. Look for opportunities to use your talents and gifts to help. In doing so, you will open more doors, some of which you really want to walk through.

**Follow-up:** Ask your mentee how they might make a new connection in which they share their talent, genuinely seeking to help further a cause (or new job) they would like to move toward. Discuss what they tried and discovered at your next meeting. Also ask them to jot a few ideas in answer to the question in the box above.

## For additional reading:

Holmes, Ryan (October 12, 2016). Inc Magazine - http://www.inc.com/ryan-holmes/move-over-millennials-5-things-you-need-to-know-about-generation-c.html

Sanborn, M. (2004). The Fred factor: How passion in your work and life can turn the ordinary into the extraordinary (1st Currency ed.). Currency/Doubleday.

Stepper, J (2015). *Working Out Loud for a Better Career and Life.* New York: Ikigai Press.

# Conversation #33

## Spirituality & Faith Traditions

**Question Preview:** *Do you have and/or practice a faith tradition? Do you feel there are things beyond what we see and observe in our everyday world? Is there a higher law? Is there a higher call?*

**Purpose:** To engage your mentee in a conversation some find difficult or even inappropriate for work, but which may challenge them to introspection. To potentially increase their acknowledgement of (and even honor for) diverse traditions among those with whom they live and work.

**Background:** My grandmother sometimes repeated an adage on social conversation:

> *"Never talk about politics, religion, or the opposite sex in polite company."*

In today's increasingly polarized environment, this idea may have more merit than ever. For that middle item—religion—I am wondering if we might make an exception in our mentoring work. Multiple research studies have shown positive mental and physical health benefits for people who practice some sort of faith tradition. As noted above, various faith traditions bring beautiful diversity to our workplaces. In addition, they are part of the tenets of diversity, equity, and inclusion. So why would we not engage in this topic?

In a previous entry, I wrote about my cancer diagnosis, surgery, and recovery. I mentioned leaning on my personal faith tradition to aid in that process. In addition to my tradition, I was mentally and physically heartened when colleagues from other faiths (and a few who did not practice any religion) sent me notes, encouragement, prayers, and energy in their own way. It was wonderfully uplifting.

In a comprehensive review of hundreds of studies, Koenig (2012) found research clearly shows people with more religion and/or spirituality have better physical and mental health and recover more quickly from health problems. Other studies have linked adults' religious involvement to better health and well-being outcomes, including lower risk of premature death (Sweeney, 2018). Within this context, let's talk about faith.

**Discussion:** Psychologists, medical doctors, leadership researchers, wisdom writers, philosophers, rabis, pastors, imams, gurus, and others have long observed that people inherently yearn for a purpose-driven life. We want to do or serve something beyond our personal goals and economic self-interest. We want to be remembered for doing something good during our lifetime.

But where does that come from? Some say religion may fill the human need for finding meaning, sparing us from existential angst while also supporting social organization (Azar, 2010). These questions are difficult. Some have noted that since we cannot answer many questions that arise about life and death, how would we know where an intrinsic longing comes from?

Whether out of deference, fear of causing offense, or fear of looking ignorant, many people today leave spirituality and religion out of conversations. However, since the Pew Research Institute estimates over five billion people in this world follow a faith tradition, I believe it is time for the discussion.

**Metacognition Minder:** A big part of mentoring is helping people be more effective in reaching their goals and life mission. By having these discussions, we can find personal growth and fulfillment as well. I urge you to engage fully and sincerely. Ask yourself these questions. Challenge yourself in the process.

**Continued Discussion:** What does it mean to have faith in a spiritual sense? Some people see faith or religion as another way of knowing, empirically tested and verified by the observable fruits of love and action. There are changed lives that attest to something unseen. These are powerful arguments and evidence. On the other hand, others contend there is no need or room for the spiritual. I have been challenged to learn about atheism and agnosticism so I can better relate to more viewpoints. I have come to appreciate all views. They help me understand mine.

With the thought of bringing people together and bridging divides, I recently undertook a study of 17th century philosopher and mathematician Blaise Pascal. In his posthumously published manuscript, *Pensées*, he posited the idea of a wager, "betting" that there is a God. I like how he toyed with this existential question. I especially appreciate how his thinking points to an approach for living that I think is difficult to debate.

A lot of people thoroughly misunderstand the nuance of his wager idea. In short, Pascal reasoned that even if there is no creator or God, if we live as if there were, we will have a better life while alive here on Earth by following the general moral conventions of caring for others, respecting life and property, and etc. These ideals are repeated in numerous belief systems. Conversely, if God is truly real, we need not fear death. We gain some sort of life for eternity when we trust therein.

Here's the disconnect: Most people focus on the wager—the bet—thinking Pascal is hedging. In doing so, we completely miss his actual thesis: *We don't have to wait till we die to win the bet.* We can have life and love and completeness now, essentially creating our own paradise here on Earth while we are physically alive. It's a fascinating idea. In early 1971, John Lennon intoned the concept: *"Imagine all the people, living life in peace."*

Discuss these questions with your mentee:

**Do you have and/or practice a faith tradition?**

**Do you feel there are things beyond what we see and observe in our everyday world?**

**Is there a higher law?**

**Is there a higher call?**

**Summary:** Regardless of your faith tradition, spiritual practice, or contentment with not needing a religious construct, Pascal's notion of practicing kindness and love and care for others in this world pays rich benefits (personally and societally) here and now. We can make our world a better place. If we or those we mentor choose to practice this other centricity in a faith tradition, we should embrace it. At the very least, encourage those you mentor to be open and respectful of deep convictions held by others, especially when they are different from ours.

Challenge your mentee with these final questions:

**How might learning about (and acknowledging) various faith traditions enrich our workplaces?**

**Whether you have a strong faith tradition, or none, could you be open to discussing topics (such as the purpose of life) that are very meaningful to many? How might these discussions strengthen our work culture and objectives?**

Bottom line: talking about faith can be a positive experience. Don't forget that the physical and mental health benefits are real.

## For additional reference / reading:

Azar, B. (2010). A reason to believe. *APA Monitor on Psychology*. Vol 41, No. 11. Available at: https://www.apa.org/monitor/2010/12/believe

Koenig HG. Religion, spirituality, and health: the research and clinical implications. ISRN Psychiatry. 2012 Dec 16;2012:278730. doi: 10.5402/2012/278730. PMID: 23762764; PMCID: PMC3671693.

Sweeney, C. (2018). Religious upbringing linked to better health and well-being during early adulthood. Harvard University, School of Public Health. Available at: https://www.hsph.harvard.edu/news/press-releases/religious-upbringing-adult-health/

 **Conversation #34**

### Changing Perspective: Embracing the Art of Possibility

**Question Preview:** *How do things look from your perspective? Might they be different (better or worse) if you could change the view? Is an improved outcome possible?*

**Purpose:** To help your mentee remember to consider their own, internal, inherent perspective when faced with an issue, or when trying to add diversity and generate ideas.

**Background:** We all know our perspective can be biased. In fact, it is. We naturally see things from our point of view. This is, of course, limited. One of the easiest things that will expand possibility is to simply change or broaden our perspective. How do we do that?

In *The Art of Possibility*, Rosamund and Benjamin Zander ask us to consider why some people seem to achieve more and more every day, while others stall or worse, flounder. When seeing a super successful person in action, they ask outright a question I've wondered myself: *Has that person discovered some revolutionary method to open doors of possibility? How do they accomplish so much!?*

The Zanders have taken a lesson from Benjamin's experience as conductor of the Boston Philharmonic. They argue that life is a story we *conduct*, and people can achieve more than they previously deemed possible by expanding their perspective.

**The Discussion:** How does one expand their perspective? We learned with E+R=O that when an event happens, we need to press pause and engage our executive brain (responding versus reacting). While that executive brain is engaged, we need to become aware or simply remind ourselves that we're seeing whatever event only from *our* perspective.

At this point, the Zanders offer two questions (paraphrased by me) to ask your mentee:

 **What assumption might you be making (that you're not aware you're making)? This limits options, potential solutions, creativity, and possibility.**

**How might you change or reconsider your view to expand your thinking? This alters your thinking to that of possibility.**

Here are some other practical ways to ask the second question in the box above:

>  **If I were someone else (who, perhaps, had different knowledge of the situation), how might I view this?**
>
> **What might a friend (or a wise grandparent, counselor, clergy, etc.) suggest in this situation?**

In E+R=O, the *outcome* can be positive or negative. It can be constricted or expanded. By asking ourselves the assumption question, we acknowledge (and remember) that we are restricted by our own perspective. So by asking the *change question*, we shift our thinking, consider other perspectives, and open the door to much greater possibility.

In *The Fred Factor*, Mark Sanborn gives a business application in which perspective can catapult you to the front of the market. When working to create value for others, Sanborn says you can *"replace money with imagination"* and outthink the competition versus outspending them. One way to accomplish this is by consciously changing your perspective. This will expand possibilities.

**Summary:** If we can remember to press pause (E+R=O), engage our executive brain, and ask ourselves the perspective question when faced with an event, we stand to expand possibilities and positive outcomes.

## For additional reference / reading:

Sanborn, M. (2004). The Fred factor: How passion in your work and life can turn the ordinary into the extraordinary (1st Currency ed.). Currency/Doubleday.

Zander, Benjamin. 2002. The Art of Possibility. Harlow, England: Penguin Books.

# Anytime Conversation Prompts

 **Conversation #35**

### Perspective Shifting

**Purpose:** To consider *perspective* more deeply and challenge your mentee to consciously employ perspective shifting *on a daily basis.*

**Background:** In prior conversations, we have talked about *changing* your perspective. Now it's time to go deeper in the challenge. *Shifting* perspective can be one of the most powerful devices in anyone's personal or professional tool kit. True perspective shifting opens our eyes to more diverse, unique, and creative solutions to problems. It unlocks doors and identifies sometimes hidden possibility. This works both personally and professionally.

What does this perspective shifting really mean? We are creatures of habit. Our brains are conditioned to our personal reality, our own singular-sighted perspective. So how can we get out of our comfort zone and discover a different way of thinking, a new approach that might move us more quickly toward our goal? Like crossing our arms the "wrong" way, it might be uncomfortable at first. But when we challenge ourselves to be open to new, more diverse ideas and ways of thinking, new possibilities arise.

*Conversations to Use Anytime*

Use the questions below as an exercise to try to change or expand perspective. Ask your mentee to think of a problem they are facing, or a difficult decision they need to make.

**Problem or decision:**
_____

**Is my thinking about this a fact, or is it my opinion? (How might someone else look at it?)**

**Challenge Q: Humility plays a role in this scenario. What are two ways to increase humility or to be open to other ideas or approaches?**

**Problem or decision:**
_____

**If I could be 5 years in the future looking back at this issue, what might I see?**

**Challenge Q: Projecting your vision into the future is pure perspective. Do you think you could deploy this approach during a stressful event? Describe how you might do that.**

**Problem or decision:**
_____

**Am I noticing the storyline in my own mind around this issue? (Could you shift the narrative or your interpretation to open new possibilities?) Jot down a few ideas on how you might do that.**

**Conversation #36**

## The Charles Schulz Mentoring Challenge: Embracing Contentment

**Question Preview:** *What and who do we really remember when it comes to things that matter?*

**Purpose:** To help your mentee remember that some things, people, and places are more meaningful than others. This conversation aims to help your mentee refocus on what matters, find contentment, and inspire you both.

**The Discussion:** Have you been feeling successful lately? Or not so much? Are you accomplishing everything you want in your job? Are you getting those promotions and raises? Or do you wish you made a little more money? Do you wish you had more recognition?

In today's world, it's easy to get off track or focus on things that lead to dissatisfaction. This can sneak up on us. We often don't even notice it has happened. We see others who appear more wealthy, healthy, or successful, and our personal contentment with life drops. Is there a way to refocus?

A number of years ago, a short exercise that challenged people to refocus on the important parts of life circulated widely via social media. Many attributed it to Charles Schulz, the creator of the Peanuts comic strip. Whether he said it or only inspired it, Schulz often included philosophy into his work and brilliantly challenged astute readers to peer beyond the cartoon characters and think deeply about life.

Here is my version of the quiz. Please try it, and share it with someone you are mentoring.

>  **Jot down one or two responses for each question:**
>
> 1. Name one or two of the wealthiest people in the world.
> 2. Name the last couple of Heisman trophy winners.
> 3. Name the last few Academy Award winners for best actor and actress.
> 4. Name the last few years of World Series or Super Bowl winners.

OK, how did you do? Most folks have difficulty in answering all those questions. The headlines of yesterday fade quickly. Even big achievements by famous people are soon forgotten. Money and recognition do not lead to being contented in life.

With this in mind, here is a different challenge to work through.

>  **Supply one or two responses to these questions:**
>
> 1. List one or two teachers who made a positive impact on you.
> 2. Name a friend who helped you through a difficult time.
> 3. Name some people who taught you something worthwhile.
> 4. Think of a few people who have made you feel appreciated and special.
> 5. Think of three people you enjoy spending time with.

How did you do on this one? Was it easier?

The lesson is clear: The people who have influence in our lives should not be the famous or rich or powerful. The people who have influence in our lives should be the ones who care about us and invest time in things that matter: *Being a friend. Teaching. Giving encouragement. Sharing joy.* These are the things that lead to becoming more gratified with our lives. Comparing ourselves to the rich and recognized—including perhaps our neighbors with a bigger house or newer car—leads only to discontentment.

When we shift our focus to things that matter and invest in other people, it is recognized. That's the kind of recognition that matters. The authentic, caring person who focuses on what matters is practicing great leadership. This will be noticed and may result in advancement in your workplace.

**Summary:** The next time you are feeling down or if you're feeling you're not accomplishing very much by the world's standards, refocus and remember this second list. THEN, *go out and become one of these people on someone else's list.*

**Metacognition Minder:** This is the key part of the challenge. This is where becoming a mentor to someone can be so impactful (Woolworth, 2019). This is the part that will propel you forward and cause you to make an amazing, positive, and life-changing impact on another person.

And here's the best part: Doing that will, in turn, make an amazing, positive, and life-changing impact on you.

**Follow-up:** For this module, make a homework assignment. Ask your mentee this key question:

### *Are you mentoring anyone?*

Challenge them to identify someone they could encourage. Challenge them to make the effort, assuring them that in doing so, they will benefit as well.

## For additional reference / reading:

Harvard Business Review (Aug. 9, 2019) – by Rick Woolworth. Great Mentors Focus on the Whole Person, Not Just Their Career. Available at: https://hbr.org/2019/08/great-mentors-focus-on-the-whole-person-not-just-their-career

# Conversation #37

## Building Trust

**Question Preview:** As we move through life, there is one question everyone asks at some level: *"Can I trust you?"*

**Purpose:** To help your mentee understand and grow their trust.

**The Discussion:** Whether we recognize this or not, when we encounter people at work, in social situations, or even within our own family, we are being evaluated as to how much others can trust us. It is not always a conscious, top of mind thought. But assuredly, our interactions are improved or impoverished based on how others perceive our trustworthiness.

Consultant and visual storyteller Tanmay Vora says, *"Trust is not something you demand, it is something you have to earn."* The way to earn trust is by having clear intentions, taking action that supports those intentions, and, most importantly, acting with the utmost integrity through human connection. Vora also notes we must realize that doing these things consistently is key because, *"Trust is built one step at a time."*

This begs the question: *What steps do we take to build trust?* Here are two challenge questions to kickstart thinking. Ask those you mentor these questions:

>  **Can the people you work with, your friends, and your family trust you?**
>
> **What have you done (and what are you doing) to earn or expand that trust?**

Let your mentee ponder these questions. Listen to some of their ideas. Discuss variables. Then, share the four benchmarks Greene and Howe (2011) put forth that measure trustworthiness. Here is what we must consider:

> **Credibility** – Can people trust the words we speak based on our knowledge or credentials? This is the most fundamental (and least involved) level of trust.
>
> **Reliability** – Do we do what we say we will do? Are we dependable to our team (or friends, family, etc.)?
>
> **Intimacy** – Can people feel safe and secure with information they share with us? We would never violate a confidentiality or embarrass anyone. This is the highest level.
>
> But these must be weighed against one's **self-orientation.** i.e., What is their primary focus? Is it on his or herself, or on others? For example, there could be someone we do not put much trust in because they seem to be overly concerned with how they appear. This is the inverse and must be factored. The overarching question we must ask ourselves and our mentees is this:
>
> *What is our self-orientation?*

**Follow-up:** Ask your mentee what they think about these ideas. Challenge them to jot down one or two things (action items) they can do this coming week to build trust with a friend, work team, or family. Ask them to share next time.

## For additional reading:

Greene, C. & Howe, A. (2011). The Trusted Advisor Fieldbook: A Comprehensive Toolkit for Leading with Trust. http://trustedadvisor.com/why-trust-matters/understanding-trust/understanding-the-trust-equation

Vora, Tanmay (March 7, 2023). Three Levels of Trust in Relationships. Available at: https://qaspire.com/three-levels-of-trust-in-relationships/

# Conversation #38

## The Power of Vision: An Indispensable Skill

**Question Preview:** Have you ever thought about how you might bring the power of visioning to a small team or an organization to help them see the future (or the way to finish a project!)?

**Purpose:** To help your mentee understand how summarizing a concept and casting a vision of it can make them indispensable to their organization.

**Background:** Teams, organizations, and even individuals often get stuck on a variety of things for various reasons. One powerful mechanism that can un-stick a group is to help members see a vision of the future – where you're going and what is possible.

Leadership guru Andy Stanley says stating a vision is a way of describing a *preferred* future. It is a mental picture of *what could be*. But realize too that it's fueled by a *conviction* that it *should* be. People and organizations often do not pause long enough to summarize where a project is going by describing a clear, simple vision of that future state. Sometimes, they just need to be reminded to do it.

Open your discussion with these prompting questions:

> **Think of an example when you saw someone cast a vision of the future. (Not science fiction or our nation's economy, but a vision of a tangible program or initiative at your workplace.)**
>
> **Describe the situation. i.e., What did they do to get others on board? How did they capture attention and help people see the potential?**

**The Discussion:** How might you bring the power of visioning to a small team or an organization to help them see the future? It's a matter of drilling down to find their *why* and then providing clarity. I have worked for more than twenty-five years at The Ohio State University in our Extension outreach. We are part of the national Land Grant system whose charge since 1862 has been to *extend* teaching out from the university center to the people.

I have been in hundreds of meetings where we're caught up on designing a new program or developing a curriculum, only to be stymied by a myriad of details that may or may not be all that important. But during those meetings, when we (*if* we) pause and drill down to the *why*, there is a powerful, palpable energy shift, and we quickly devise our path forward. For our Extension outreach, our *why* is simply to help people use knowledge to improve their lives. Focusing on that can direct our incremental action steps (e.g., program development). This can get lost, so we often need the reminder.

Here's a question for your mentee to ponder:

> **Could you develop the skill of observing, clarifying, and describing a vision of the potential future? Remember, this can be done at an individual, team, or even organizational scale.**

**Here's an approach:** When stuck or stymied during a meeting, press pause. Remind folks of *what could be*. Remember, this should be fueled by a *conviction* of what *should* be.

1. Summarize the big concepts. State them simply. Stanley says, *"Memorable is portable."* Keep it short. It's about what, not how. (You'll circle back to the *how*.)
2. Cast the vision convincingly. State the problem and offer a solution. The key is to explain why (drilling to the biggest why).

*Here are some vision statements I've looked up from the Internet:*

- ALS Association: A world without ALS.
- ONE Campaign: To make poverty history.
- Habitat for Humanity: A world where everyone has a decent place to live.

**Summary:** If you can help people (or a team or an organization) clearly see the mission and vision, their detail work expands exponentially because they tie it to the higher purpose (the bigger *why*). This can be powerful for any group.

Work with your mentee on the idea of visioning. Challenge them to find opportunities to *summarize* and *clarify* a concept or future focus on a project team or in their home. Ask them to share an example if/when they try it. Follow up with questions they encounter.

## For additional reference / reading:

Stanley, Andy (2016). *Making Vision Stick*. Leadercast 2016: Architects of Tomorrow. Available at: https://youtu.be/zAOg_rGVlr4

**Conversation #39**

## Storytelling: A Useful Tool in Any Career

**Question Preview:** *If connection is critical to career success, could storytelling enhance your opportunities?*

**Purpose:** To illustrate how telling stories can be a powerful means of helping your mentee make connections, support their work, and advance organizational mission attainment.

**Background:** We all know a few people who are natural storytellers. Sometimes, we wish they would not tell so many, or that they would learn to shorten them up a bit. But have you considered how storytelling can be a useful tool in your work and life?

Early in my career, I spent a half-dozen years with a Fortune 500 company in the paper industry. There, I saw smart engineers and managers often giving one-way streams of information or direction to union workers, and I saw brilliant union workers attempting to share production information with management. Most often, I saw frustrated people on both sides because their conversations did not take the time to share the *why*. Telling a worker to do something differently without giving context is detrimental to your objective. Telling a manager that something you're trying is not working is okay, but they need to know *why*. That is critical. If we can include storytelling in the mix, communication in both directions becomes enhanced, and your objective stands a much greater chance of being achieved.

**The Discussion:** So how might stories help us in our work? This is a straightforward concept. When we tell stories in the traditional sense, we *create narrative* which is a social science construct. We focus on sense-making, morals, instruction, or perhaps an aesthetic. We weave concepts and subject material to engage in some way. The story helps our audience(s) focus on the content, providing a place to begin inquiry. Ultimately, they provide the *why*.

Return with me to the early 1990s and my paper industry days. There, I quickly learned that if we could include a quick story of *why* some change was needed, both union papermakers and engineer managers would quickly adopt the process and begin making progress. It just wasn't that complicated. But it took focus and deliberate attention to make it happen.

Here are some points on storytelling that can be useful to anyone (particularly your mentees) working to make positive change happen (or respond to events) in the workplace. Adding stories will move you toward mission attainment.

### *Storytelling:*

- *Stories are illustrative.*
- *Stories provide context and perspective.*
- *Stories can make the abstract concrete.*
- *Stories can move us (emotionally, and physically) to action.*

[See my section on andragogy (adult learning theory) which illustrates how adults need context to engage.]

Here's a question to ponder:

 **When might you need to use storytelling to convey an important message?**

Here's a brief story from several years ago when my work organization, OSU Extension, was making a request to the Ohio legislature for continued funding for our 4-H youth development program. We highlighted some statistics (e.g., that we annually serve over 240,000 young people in all of Ohio's 88 counties, and that we serve youth with disabilities through Special Needs Camps and other accommodating programs). But it was one mom with one story that caught the attention of everyone. Her testimony was simple, but extraordinarily powerful:

> *"Every other youth organization turned us away. They didn't have the capacity, or they didn't want to deal with my son's disability. But when we tried 4-H, they welcomed us. My son found a place to belong."*

This example makes it easy to understand why stories are so powerful.

Remember this. The most important stories are not the stories you tell about yourself or your program, product, or service. The most important stories are those going on inside the heads of your audience: your workers, clients, partners, funders. The ones they are telling themselves affect how they view the world as well as your information or current request. Their counter-story will influence the decisions they make. So maintain awareness and listen for their responses or reactions.

**Summary:** This begs the question: *How do we reach people and capture their attention when needing to move them to action?* The simple answer is to start with context – the *why*. If our audiences understand the *why*, we have built the connection and made a partnership. The *why* is everything. Storytelling helps you explain and promote that *why*. This will yield positive results.

**Follow-up:** Ask your mentee if they think storytelling could aid them in their work. Ask for an example.

## Conversation #40

### Leading with Humility

**Question Preview:** *Can an attitude of humility help a leader expand potential and positive outcomes? Could inviting diverse input lead to discovery and opportunity?*

**Purpose:** To remind us that potential is expanded when we lead with humility.

**Background:** It is reported that Frank Lloyd Wright defined an expert as *"someone who has stopped thinking because he knows."* We all know that person. Or maybe several. If they are leading a team, organization, volunteer project, or (this last one might be uncomfortable) a family, they could improve outcomes if they'd simply stop talking and invite others to provide input.

The painful question we all must ask ourselves is this: *How often do I think I'm the expert?* (Ouch.)

There are, of course, people who are blessed with ability, insight, and wisdom. Please see the note of caution included below that I sent to one of my highly talented undergrad students in 2020. I fully believe he will become an expert in his career endeavors. My note to him includes a suggestion for how he might consciously show humility in his future.

For this conversation, here's an initial question for discussion with your mentee.

> **Can an attitude of humility help a leader expand potential and positive outcomes? Describe how that might work.**

**The Discussion:** In 2013, Former MIT professor Edgar Schein published *Humble Inquiry*. Later that year in a video from the IBM Zurich Research Center in Rüschlikon, Schein asked how an organization can get all the bosses (leaders) to create a climate where those under them feel free to engage. He said upward communication is often lacking in business, but leaders could make strides if they did three things:

1. Do less telling.
2. Learn to do more asking.
3. Do a better job of listening and acknowledging.

Schein claims that if we wish to find our own *original, individualized answers* (solutions to problems), then we will be required to do a deeper kind of search. In other words, our human *experience* is a necessary component of adult learning, knowledge synthesis, and the ultimate application.

What does this mean for us today? In brief, when we face challenging questions, Schein suggests we *"live with the question"* for a bit. Sleep on it. Allow our imaginations and our brain power time to work while also inviting naïve questions. Those naïve questions can be the best kind because they look at the issue with a beginner's mind and ask about the fundamentals. Again, the experts are often too close to the subject to see what they're missing, or (as in Wright's quote) they quit thinking or asking because they believe they already have the answer.

**Questions to ponder:**

**What is a current project where you might do less telling and more listening?**

**How might your team (or colleagues or family) respond?**

- Might they become more creative?
- Might they take more ownership?
- Might they grow personally or professionally by being permitted to try even if they fail?

**How can you use "humble inquiry" to expand potential and positive outcomes?**

**Could inviting diverse input lead to the discovery of opportunity?**

**Summary:** Ask your mentee what they think about Schein's approach. Let the conversation unfold. Go deep by prodding for personal examples.

**Follow-up:** Ask your mentee what they think about approaching their own leadership with humility. For your next meeting, ask them to bring an example of a time when they had a choice to inquire and listen, or to talk. How did they respond?

~ ~ ~

***A note of advice to a highly talented student:***

Dear "Collin"

I made a note today in your paper about your remarkable level of understanding and insight... And I truly mean it. It will take you a few years to even begin understanding how valuable your combination of technical skills and insight are. But it will come.

But I offer a note of caution: Gifts like this will require some serious reflection on humility in the future. As you grow in your career (and begin getting invited to do cool things, join teams, increase responsibility and salary, etc. etc.) ... it could get a little heady. Maintaining curiosity and a continuous-learning mindset helps. In short, curious folks acknowledge that there's always more to learn… and there are others (including people without degrees) who have vast experiential, cultural, and historic knowledge. Being open and remembering that can be helpful.

It's also helpful to know/remember that IQ, EQ, and talent inherently come with a lot of responsibility. However, it's NOT ALL ON YOUR SHOULDERS. We're made for community. We're made to connect and to share our various talents to collectively make the world a better place. So you don't have to carry the load alone. (i.e., don't be a perfectionist or beat yourself up over the failures that will certainly come! Learn. Then move ahead using the missteps as data.)

I've probably only ever given this kind of "warning" to two or three students before. . . people in whom I've recognized remarkable abilities or gifts. I hope you take it as my highest compliment.

I believe success in life is making the grocery clerk smile. It's lying to the hotel staff… telling them how good the free breakfast is (but sincerely showing how appreciative you are of THEIR work). It's also bringing your insight and creativity to a team. But it's MOSTLY bringing a smile or kind word to those teammates.

Whether you get a great or crappy job… and whether you make a lot or a little money… success and joy will come in sharing your great talents throughout your life. Like love, the more you give away, the more you get in return. And the better our world becomes because of you. It's a remarkable thing.

I wish you well "Collin." My hopes and prayers are for you to have real, purposed, fulfilling success in life.

## 20 Bonus Questions to Use Anytime

**Purpose:** To consider questions that take us deeper. These are for pondering anytime (with a friend, or in our own brain).

**Background:** Great questions can powerfully move people to act, to get un-stuck, and to see potential. These questions are conversation-starters that I have collected over many years. Choose one or two for additional mentoring conversations. Challenge yourself to go deep on some of these. They can help you personally and professionally.

1. What is the world teaching you right now?
2. When have you made an impact that you felt was significant?
3. What would a close friend say your strengths are? (Do you agree?)
4. How might you further develop your strengths?
5. What does success look like for you? What can you do really well that will help you get there?
6. What obstacles are you facing?
7. What are you not doing that might be keeping you from success?
8. What can you control (versus what can you NOT control?) What options might you deploy?
9. Think about a time when you felt like you failed. How did you bounce back? What did you actually do? (In the short-term, and over time?)
10. Describe a recent setback. How are you recovering?
11. What leadership skills would you like to develop?
12. Who was the best teacher you ever had? Explain why.
13. Is there anything you pretend you understand, but you really don't? How might you gain understanding?
14. When you were a little kid, what did you REALLY like doing? Can you capture the spirit or essence of that today in your work?
15. If you were NOT here right now (in your job, etc.), what would you be doing? Like RIGHT NOW?
16. If you could have really high skill in one area, what would it be? Why?

17. If you could invite anyone living or dead to dinner, who would it be?
18. What are you reading?
19. Where do you need the most help? Where can you get help?
20. What topic have you not explored? What would you like to explore?

**Homework:** Have those you mentor reflect on these perspective questions from time to time. What subjects or areas might they wish to explore further in reading or study? Pick out three or four questions that resonate. Circle or highlight them. Set additional meeting times to go deeper and continue the conversations.

# Section 4

# Teaching & Engagement Strategies

## Teaching for Connection and Engagement in Mentoring

Mentoring is a form of teaching. This section provides outlines of proven teaching practice that will result in stronger engagement in your mentoring. Please know this, you need not undertake formal study in teaching to find success. Simply gaining an understanding of the *teaching process*—what's happening behind the scenes as teaching (or mentoring) takes place—will greatly aid your ability to engage in these conversations and achieve positive growth for your mentee. I remember sitting front row in a faculty meeting when former Ohio State University President Michael V. Drake said, *"Our best students can survive mediocre teaching. But we owe excellent teaching to all our students, especially those who struggle finding success."* I spontaneously applauded. He was describing me forty years ago. A small investment in studying teaching methods and engagement can help greatly. This works in mentoring as well.

Mentoring is also a form of leadership. Leaders are also teachers. The strategies outlined in this section will help you strengthen your own *leadership practice* no matter where your job lies in the organizational hierarchy.

The outlines below result from my investment in reading, researching, and compiling ideas for improving teaching and engagement, and then taking the time over the past dozen years to experiment and ask my audiences, *"Did this resonate?"* I have also bolstered these teaching tools by gleaning input from years of my formal teaching evaluations. Lastly, I have led two fairly recent research studies on student-teacher engagement and have expanded my suggested engagement approaches based on these data as well.

My foundational belief is that if you can help your audience (mentee, student, group, co-workers, supervisor, or even your children) reach *the intersection of theory and practice*, then they will find inspiration and success. I believe that is one of the most powerful points in mentoring. i.e., We (you, me, your mentee) may have knowledge in our brain that, for example, *changing perspectives* can help us with *problem solving*. It often takes a conversation to create the ah-ha moment where the idea or the theory is paired with a real-world example. That's what these *40 Conversations* aim to do.

You can achieve this more quickly by expanding your teaching abilities.

Again, please read through these engagement strategies. You need not become an expert, nor have a full understanding of the related teaching theory. These are very basic engagement constructs. But if you begin to understand the basics, you will improve your mentoring and teaching outcomes.

## Teaching / Engagement Strategy #1

## Reach Before You Teach: Connection Strategies for Mentors, Teachers, Coaches, Supervisors, and even Families.

**Purpose:** Effective mentoring, teaching, coaching, supervising, and leading requires connection. If you do not first engage, your message will not resonate as fully, nor will it have the impact you desire.

**Overview:** In March 2020, our oldest daughter moved her laptop, books, and lab manuals from her college dorm room to our home's dining room. I simultaneously began teaching, meeting with students, and even conducting master's thesis defenses and doctoral candidacy exams from my home desk nearby. At the time, I could not help but overhear my daughter discussing strategies with other students on how to interpret a professor's slides or how to understand a comment that may have had clarity when said in person but when given online became cryptic. I also realized that the strategic alignment and board development work I was doing as a facilitator (also online) was less dynamic, recognizing that the outcomes were not as strong or precise as I thought they could be.

During the COVID-19 pandemic, our entire national education system shifted to online instruction. At the same time, many businesses began or dramatically expanded the grand experiment of remote work. Some of this was seamless; most was not. These observations led me to investigate connection and engagement strategies that could be deployed as the pandemic persisted.

Over many late nights reading, I devised an idea of mashing up classic leadership theory and strategy with teaching praxis to help us *reach* students before attempting to *teach* them. The theory applied to and worked very well with my business, local government, nonprofit, and other academic clients, as well as with individuals I was personally coaching and mentoring at The Ohio State University.

This online engagement required some reconfiguration of teaching methods to achieve higher reaches. For example, adopting Bloom's Taxonomy enabled students to advance from remembering and understanding, moving them toward application, analysis, and evaluation of our lessons in the context of our world. This approach required modifying my tried-and-true strategic process outlines as well. The key was that we needed to first meet our students and clients where *they* were… *and* where *we* were as well. Only then could we engage with efficiency and success.

**NOTE:** Though most teaching and business operations have returned to in-person formats, this approach still works. It also works as a hybrid. Most importantly, connecting first resonates. Thus, I have continued to use this ***reach before you teach*** approach at the start of *all* my in-person, online, and hybrid work even today.

**Applying Leadership Theory:**

As noted, I imagined mashing up leadership theory with teaching. The approach I landed on modified a leadership philosophy from Jim Kouzes and Barry Posner. I adapted the idea to bring a leadership perspective to our engagement, whatever the context. Kouzes and Posner (2015) suggest five practices of leadership that can optimize relationships. Though outlined for business, these may be applied when teaching, coaching, or mentoring.

I have outlined ideas for teaching and mentoring below, following their five practices. Again, this ties back to the key idea that we must *reach before we teach.*

### 1. Model the Way:

I have heard former Ohio State running back and two-time Heisman Trophy winner Archie Griffin say on several occasions, *"Adopt an attitude of gratitude."* Tell your students or those you are mentoring you're thankful for the opportunity to work with them. Tell them out loud during your Zoom or while meeting in person that you recognize they are bringing unique backgrounds, knowledge, and resources—some things you don't know—and that you want this relationship to be a two-way street. Explicitly tell them that you want to learn and grow *with* them. In doing this, you are modeling the way, sending a humble message that acknowledges their life and voice matter and have great value. This is a tremendously powerful and positive message.

### 2. Inspire a Shared Vision:

Gary Burnison, Korn Ferry CEO, says when things are going well, people look to a leader for validation. But when there's difficulty, they look to a leader for reassurance. He contends that leadership is connecting the dots so people (our students or mentees in this case) can see and be reassured about where we're going.

In teaching and mentoring in-person or online, sharing a vision of where you're going (with every interaction) is important. Tying together disparate elements, concepts, or processes—and reiterating the *big picture* more frequently—is important, particularly when mentoring relationships are often limited on how often you can meet. By including exercises and reflections like the tools outlined in this book, you can help your mentees contextualize the ideas and questions you're asking and better understand *where theory meets practice.* That's the sweet spot.

## 3. Challenge the Process:

In 2020, the shift to online instruction, business, mentoring, and other activity was prescribed. Today, many mentoring programs are prescribed as well. Some are prepackaged and have varying levels of effectiveness. Others are highly formal which, according to some studies, can result in almost zero effectiveness because the requirements (designed to build relationships) disrupt real relationship building.

Regardless of the mentoring process, might we loosen our grip on what we think is the right way, and challenge that prescribed process a bit? Could we allow our mentees to suggest options or variations? If we give them permission, they may well suggest innovative approaches that will increase engagement, learning, and personal and professional growth. Even if you are using this *Encouraging Mentor* tool kit for example, you could invite them to choose every other conversation topic. This blends into the next section, enabling others to act.

## 4. Enable Others to Act:

How can you help your mentees feel strong, capable, informed, and connected, whether online or in person? One of the best ways I have observed is through fostering collaboration. Encourage introductions and dialogue with other individuals and teams. Build trust with and among your mentees by being more open and transparent. Then let go and let them grow.

## 5. Encourage the Heart:

This is the most important and critical item on the list. Caring is at the heart of teaching and mentoring. During the extraordinary and fearful time of the pandemic, students and mentees needed reassurance. They needed our calm and steady leadership. And they needed to know we were in it together. Today, this has not changed, especially in mentoring relationships.

In summary, along with Kouzes and Posner's *five practices* we can and should also consider deploying other leadership models as we engage in mentoring. You have most likely heard of these theories (highlighted below in bold). I encourage you to do some reading on each. It can be very instructive and can help you see potential you can encourage in those you are mentoring.

Here are some examples:

- How might you bolster your mentee's ***charismatic leadership*** traits?
- How might you encourage them to embrace ***servant leadership*** to ensure they recognize the potential for making a difference in their organization or world?
- Can you use the leadership constructs of ***authenticity and transparency*** to show mentees you care and are in this with them?
- Can you show ***intellectual humility*** when mentoring or delivering instruction? Might you invite a co-creation of knowledge?

**Summary:** Being an effective mentor or teacher requires nuanced and (I contend) advanced forms of leadership. Are you willing to give some of these a try? This other-centric approach may pay dividends you don't expect. Remember, *reach before you teach.*

## For additional reference / reading:

Burnison, Gary (March 29, 2020). *Everything will be OK.* Korn Ferry marketing correspondence.

Kouzes, J.M. & Posner, B.Z. (2012). The Leadership Challenge (5th ed.). John Wiley & Sons.

# Teaching / Engagement Strategy #2

# Connection Before Content

**Purpose:** The title says it all. We must connect with our mentees or other audiences before delivering or attempting to teach any content. The *best* approach uses a connection activity that relates to the content.

**Overview:**

*"Let's give it just a few more minutes and then we'll get started."*

How many times have you heard a meeting leader or facilitator say that? Whether you are in an online or in-person meeting, those words literally have the effect of disrespecting everyone who has arrived or logged in on time. In short, the teacher or meeting facilitator is rewarding those who are late by holding everyone else up. Sound a bit harsh? That's intentional. I contend we need to demonstrate respect for our audiences, and it begins with honoring the majority who have mutually respected others by arriving on time. It also begins with making a deliberate connection prior to jumping in.

Let's return to my favorite connection and engagement guru, Chad Littlefield (http://weand.me) who helps organizations around the globe strengthen connections so they can move toward mission attainment. The key to beginning any conversation or meeting is to do something Littlefield calls a *Connection Before Content* experiment. This can be as simple as asking an intriguing question or creating some kind of personal interaction. As noted, the prompt *should* relate to your topic. That's key for going deep.

Whether online or in-person, as people are entering the room, post a question on the board, in the chat box, on a slide, or in screen-share to initiate the connection. This simple activity will stimulate brain neurotransmitters and literally jump-start engagement with the content that is forthcoming.

Below are some examples borrowed or modified from Littlefield's *Unofficial Start* outline. Try them with your mentee. Use them in a group meeting. Throw one out to your teenager! You can catch even *their* attention. I also recommend further reading and watching videos at Chad's website. He has a remarkable collection of engagement strategies therein.

**Engagement Questions:**

1. What is one thing life is teaching you right now?
2. What is one of your favorite places in the world? Why?
3. Do you have a bucket list? What's on it?
4. What's something you've always wanted to learn?
5. Tell about a time you learned from a failure.
6. What brings you joy?
7. What's a favorite memory in life?
8. What is something you lost… and something you gained because of COVID?

## For additional reference / reading:

Littlefield, Chad (2020). *The Unofficial Start* – Available at http://weand.me

## Teaching / Engagement Strategy #3

## Recognizing Potential

**Purpose:** To help you recognize potential in mentees or students, and to think about ways to deliberately communicate what you recognize.

**The Discussion:** In the introductory section of this book, I noted that observation might be the most important thing a mentor can do. I suggested you try to see in your mentee *something that has not been made manifest to the rest of the world… yet.* I asked you to consider what spark they possess that needs fanning to become a flame.

In another conversation tool, I suggested watching the brief Crystal Williams video. In it, she urges us to recognize something in others–their potential–perhaps before they recognize it in themselves. It is a powerful talk. I highly recommend pausing right now and watching it again: https://youtu.be/-OdTCazBFo0.

In two Harvard Business Review articles, researchers list overlapping traits that help us recognize high potential in an individual. In the first, Chamorro-Premuzic, Adler, and Kaiser (2017) name three general markers:

1. **Ability:** Can they do the job? Do they demonstrate knowledge and skill needed to perform key tasks?
2. **Social skills:** How are their working relationships? How is their EQ, specifically their ability to manage themselves?
3. **Drive:** Do they have high motivation to work hard?

In the second article, Fernández-Aráoz suggests assessing potential of aspiring managers by *"checking their motivational fit"* and then rating them on four key hallmarks. These are:

1. **Curiosity:** Do they seek new experiences, knowledge, and feedback? Are they open to change?
2. **Insight:** Can they gather and interpret information to leverage it to cast a future vision? *(clarity)*
3. **Engagement:** Do they use emotion and logic to connect with people? *(EQ)*
4. **Determination:** Is their focus on the mission despite any challenges? Can they bounce back from adversity?

**Summary:** All these citations point to one thing: *recognizing potential.* Observing and naming the spark you see in a mentee or student can help them find a path, career advancement, or a strength they did not (yet) recognize themselves. Our job is to look for these things. Identify them. Then let your mentee or student know what you see. It will encourage them more than you might imagine. It can change their life for the better. As I noted, those changes can ripple out to their family, friends, coworkers, and networks. Your observation and encouragement could start a sequence of events that can change the *world* for the better.

**Homework:** Observe and identify a spark in someone you're mentoring, a student, coworker, or even someone in your family. Consider their potential. Jot down some ideas. Then share those with them.

## For additional reading:

Chamorro-Premuzic, T., Adler, S., and Kaiser, R. (2017). What Science Says About Identifying High-Potential Employees. Harvard Business Review. Available from: https://hbr.org/2017/10/what-science-says-about-identifying-high-potential-employees

Fernández-Aráoz, C., Roscoe, A., and Aramaki, K. (2017). Turning Potential into Success: The Missing Link in Leadership Development. Harvard Business Review. Available from: https://hbr.org/2017/11/turning-potential-into-success-the-missing-link-in-leadership-development

Williams, Crystal (2021). Stories from the Stage, March 1, 2021: https://youtu.be/-OdTCazBFo0

## Teaching / Engagement Strategy #4

## Creating Serendipity; Believing in Your Mentee

**Question Preview:** How can you recognize potential in those you mentor? How might you deliberately communicate what you recognize, and articulate how you believe in them?

**Purpose:** To purposefully create meaningful moments in which you speak encouragement to those you mentor.

**The Discussion:** Think back to when you were in college. Can you recall a time when a professor (or a friend) encouraged you? Perhaps they said you were a good writer. Or maybe they complimented your science or math abilities.

> *I (personally) have no memory of anything like that. I wasn't the best student; and I seriously considered dropping out on several occasions. I simply did not have any vision for the future apart from making enough money to drive a cool car. But I distinctly recall my supervisor in the OSU Main Library, Maureen Donovan, who implanted some radical ideas in my head during what she probably saw as casual conversation.*

> *First, she invited me back as her work-study student for all four years of my undergraduate experience. She said I did a really good job. Second, she told me I should think about getting my MLS (Master of Library Science) because she thought I'd be a really great librarian. Yes, my family had encouraged me over the years; but here was a real professional with advanced degrees saying I had potential. This was something entirely new. Wow.*

Please note, Maureen said those things to me nearly forty years ago (circa 1983-86) when I served as her student assistant. But I remember the conversation as clearly as if it were last week. I can see the room, the bookshelves, and the study desks surrounding us there on the third floor of OSU's Main Library. I can see her kind smile. At the time, neither of us would have labeled it as such, but her words **created a serendipitous moment** that changed my life for the better. *She recognized some potential in me that I did not recognize in myself.*

**The Research:** In the 2010 article, *Serendipity in Teaching and Learning: The Importance of Critical Moments,* Dr. Peter Giordano suggests professors can alter lives and help transform identities through their casual and random remarks to students.

Giordano reminds us that college students are particularly sensitive because they have moved away from parental influence and are beginning to establish their own inner authority. He also suggests that if we are attentive to this potential growth, then we can make a significant contribution to their future well-being.

Giordano says we need to *"be humbly mindful of the power we may exert over our students' development, self-authorship, and aspirations."* Whether face-to-face or in written feedback on papers or assignments our seemingly random comments can have a significant impact over time. Giordano calls it disrupting students' self-perceptions; and I would expand that notion labeling it *encouraging potential.*

So what might we do as mentors? Below are three challenge activities I hope you will try with your mentees. You may never learn if your words were impactful or not, but please do not let that stop you from trying. The potential is there.

**Challenge Activities:**

1. Consider how you can identify and lift up the potential you see in others.
2. Look for opportunities to believe in someone you are mentoring, even if they may not yet believe in themself. Then tell them.
3. Watch Crystal Williams brief but powerful story about recognizing potential and believing in others: https://youtu.be/-OdTCazBFo0

## For additional reading:

Williams, Crystal (2021). Stories from the Stage, March 1, 2021: https://youtu.be/-OdTCazBFo0

Giordano, P. J. (2010). Serendipity in teaching and learning: The importance of critical moments. Journal on Excellence in College Teaching, 21 (3), 5-27.

## Teaching / Engagement Strategy #5

## Pedagogy vs. Andragogy

**Purpose:** Adult learners (your mentees) require context. A strategic use of andragogy (adult learning theory) will help.

**Overview:** Adults and youth have different learning styles and needs. The traditional one-way dissemination of information (the *sage on the stage*) is not very engaging, nor effective, for most adults. Instead, adult learning is frequently enhanced via a co-construction of knowledge. In other words, there are many *ways of knowing* such as empirical adequacy and logical consistency. But there is also experiential relevancy. The latter is where adults connect most strongly. They want to bring their knowledge to the table to explore and discover and grow with you.

I consider adult learning as ages sixteen and up. Here, context, culture, and power are highly relevant. Therefore, our approach must shift away from basic pedagogy allowing us to better meet the needs of our adult learners.

Malcolm Knowles (1984) defined andragogy as *"the art and science of helping adults learn."* He identified the six principles of adult learning:

1. Adults are internally motivated and self-directed.
2. Adults bring life experiences and knowledge to learning experiences.
3. Adults are goal oriented.
4. Adults are relevancy oriented.
5. Adults are practical.
6. Adult learners like to be respected.

I compiled the chart below based on numerous articles and research studies that distinguish the two approaches. This may be helpful in understanding how to approach those you teach, lead, or mentor.

|  | Pedagogy | Andragogy |
|---|---|---|
| The Learning | – Instructor supplies information, data, learning.<br>– Instructor responsible for content.<br>– Instructor evaluates learning. | – Learner brings experiential knowledge.<br>– Learner is responsible for learning content.<br>– Learner self-evaluates. |
| The Learning experience | – By definition, pedagogy aims at young learners.<br>– Young learners have little experience to bring or tap into.<br>– Instructor's experience is the basis. | – Life experiences are automatically brought into the experience.<br>– Other learners (e.g., colleagues / classmates) contribute diverse experiences.<br>– Experiences are a source of self-identity. |
| Readiness to learn | – Young learners (students) receive instruction that's often mandated.<br>– Mastery may be required (or desired) prior to advancing. | – The learner desires knowledge to improve some aspect of their life, or to improve performance, etc.<br>– They can assess gaps in what they know and what they need to learn. |
| The Learner's orientation | – Subject matter is often prescribed.<br>– Content is often sequenced. | – Learning is organized around life or work situations vs prescribed subject matter content.<br>– Learners desire to solve problems and learn approaches or tasks to live in a better way.<br>– Learning is based on real life needs or desires. |

| The Learner's motivation | – External / extrinsic motivation is dominate (sometimes involving competition for grades, or consequences of failure). | – Internal / intrinsic motivation dominates.<br>– Real life application drives motivation. |
|---|---|---|

**Summary:** Remember to view your adult learners as contributors to the mentoring discussion or classroom dynamic. Their experiences and diversity can enrich learning for everyone, but only if we invite that participation and have the intellectual humility to be truly open and listen. In mentoring, we must key in on these six principles so we can better engage, relate, and cement lessons.

## Teaching / Engagement Strategy #6

## Transfer of Knowledge

**Purpose:** Effective mentoring requires us to *transfer* not only information but also knowledge to our mentee. This is a specific construct included in most theories of teaching.

**Overview:** Knowledge transfer occurs when people learn to *apply* information, data, strategies, or skills to some sort of *new situation* or context. This transfer is related to the section on adult learning theory. We love context. We learn best with application. So when considering the transfer of knowledge, we must ask, *how is our mentoring ensuring this critical transfer?*

Again, Knowles' adult learning theory (1968, 1984) confirms that to be most effective, we must recognize adults 1.) are internally motivated, 2.) bring life experiences, 3.) are goal oriented, 4.) need relevance, 5.) need practicality, and 6.) wish to be respected. When designing mentoring approaches (e.g., conversations found in this book), we must incorporate at least some of these elements if we want to achieve a successful outcome.

Adults will remember more, and the transfer of learning will be highest by following this approach. This is how we can accelerate and cement learning objectives such as those outlined in Bloom's Taxonomy of Learning (1956) model. Here, we desire to move our learners from simply 1.) remembering information, to 2.) understanding it, 3.) applying it, 4.) analyzing it, 5.) evaluating it, and ultimately 6.) using it in a new way. These components fit well into the construct of mentoring.

Some approaches to enhance this process include assigning independent work, outlining ideas, storytelling, listening, and sharing potential results or outcomes to add additional learning opportunities from each and with other.

## Teaching / Engagement Strategy #7

## Recognizing 8 Smarts

**Purpose:** Each person you mentor, now or in the future, possesses different strengths when it comes to learning. Recognizing these can help you home in and better connect with your mentee, cementing lessons in real time.

**Overview:** Everyone has what Dr. Kathy Koch describes as *8 Smarts*, but we have them in differing amounts. We use them at varying levels. Thinking about these can be helpful when mentoring.

I really like how Dr. Koch reimagined Harvard psychologist Howard Gardner's multiple intelligences theory from his 1983 book *Frames of Mind*. Koch translated it into everyday language. The supposition is that everyone is smart in different ways. Knowing about, understanding, and practicing with all eight smarts helps motivation and comprehension.

Critics claim these *intelligences* simply represent talents, personality traits, and abilities. That said, recognizing and telling someone you are mentoring (perhaps someone feeling inadequate in some area) that they are still smart can be powerful. Reminding them that they have *other ways of knowing*.

Adults (as well as children) can learn how to determine which smarts are their strengths. They can learn to activate those, especially when challenged or bored. Try sharing these constructs next time you are coaching, mentoring, or teaching. This is a metacognition moment for your audience. You are helping them see the process of learning and think about their own learning. That is a good thing to do.

These are outlined for teaching. Again, teaching is the heart of mentoring. Imagine helping your mentee(s) better understand that they possess each of these smarts in varying degrees.

1. **Word smart - *thinking with words:*** These folks like words. They like reading things for comprehension, and perhaps reading aloud or rewriting important concepts.
2. **Logic smart - *thinking with questions, cause-effect, and compare-contrast relationships:*** These folks like to predict things, such as what questions will appear on a test or what might be the result if a team at work follows a certain path. They analyze what's illogical and create experiments in their brains to play out scenarios.
3. **Picture smart - *thinking with pictures:*** Many folks visualize concepts and definitions. They plot points and create displays in their minds and on paper to cement learning.
4. **Music smart - *thinking with rhythms and melodies:*** Do you remember how you learned to spell Mississippi? A lot of people use rhythms and melodies to learn and remember things. They add sing-song effects to statements they want to remember.
5. **Body smart - *thinking with touch and movement:*** In this area, facial expressions matter. People may explore real objects or draw pictures in the air with their hands. Moving helps them put the pieces together.
6. **Nature smart - *thinking with patterns:*** Some people look for patterns to activate the nature-smart part of the brain. They discover relationships and similarities among things being studied. They also may like to work or study outside.

7. **People smart - *thinking with other people:*** Do you need to talk with others, brainstorm, or react to things in groups? This is a powerful way to expand and welcome diversity into your thinking, and help you see the bigger picture. These folks understand the old adage that *two heads are better than one.*
8. **Self smart - *thinking with reflection deeply inside of ourselves:*** We sometimes think of these folks as introverts or being shy. But do not discount these deep thinkers. They relate learning to their experiences. Deep reflection is a key to mentoring.

## For additional reading:

Koch, Kathy (2016). 8 Great Smarts: Discover and Nurture Your Child's Intelligences. Moody Publishers, Chicago. Online at: http://drkathykoch.com/studying-with-all-8-smarts/

## Teaching / Engagement Strategy #8

## 12 Considerations for Engagement (Teaching Approaches for Mentoring)

**Purpose:** To help you think through varying considerations that are critical to excellent teaching. Again, you must *reach before you teach*.

**Overview:** As noted, mentoring is teaching. Below is a collection of brief annotations I put together over the years on key approaches and considerations critical to excellent teaching. Today, we will apply them to mentoring. These should be given a high priority when developing a personal teaching (mentoring) philosophy. (Hint: That is your next exercise.) These are meta-level / metacognitive ideas to hold in the back of your head when engaging with your mentee or audience.

Each of these ideas and constructs could be a semester-long course. Most of these have been life-long research portfolios for some very brilliant people. For the purposes of helping you, the mentor, gain understanding of the teaching process, I have boiled them down to the basic key ideas. Holding this background context will help in your practice of teaching and mentoring.

After studying these brief annotations, my hope is you will be prompted to go read and discover more. Do it for your mentee(s). Do it for yourself. Research shows that continuous learning promotes cognitive function and protects our brains from mental decline as we age. Continuous learning reminds us to adopt a more humble approach in our teaching and mentoring. Continuous learning will also improve our lives by equipping us to be better mentors, better teachers, and better able to enjoy our work and home lives.

Remember: Many of these are power-packed brief overviews of ideas that were years or decades in the formulation. Please investigate, read more, and go deeper.

## 1. Who is your audience? What's their perspective?

### Younger Audiences: Pre-teens through undergrads

You may be coaching or mentoring pre-teens through undergraduate age students who each has varying perspectives of **dualism, multiplicity, and relativism** (Perry, 1968). In other words, what you say and how you say it can be received with a remarkable range of comprehension, acceptance, or rejection.

- Dualism (concrete knowledge/perspectives; there is only right or wrong, good or bad)
- Multiplicity (subjective knowledge/perspectives; ambiguity exists; any opinion can be valid)
- Relativism (procedural knowledge/perspectives; acceptance of ambiguity; need to evaluate viable solutions; etc.)

A key point to remember is that people can hold these varying perspectives *on different subjects* depending on their prior knowledge, beliefs, indoctrination, family history, and personal experience. This must be considered when developing and delivering mentoring conversations. *How will you engage your mentee across varying perspectives (meeting them where they are... and challenging them to grow)?*

**Older Audiences: Teens through adult** *(noting teens overlap)*

Adults and youth have different learning styles and needs. As noted before, the traditional one-way dissemination of information is not very engaging, nor effective for most adults. In adult learning, **context, culture, and power** are highly relevant. Our teaching and mentoring approach must shift to meet these learners' needs. Reflect on Malcolm Knowles and his construct of andragogy.

When mentoring adults, you have an opportunity to talk transparently about **metacognition.** Tell your mentee you want them to think about their thinking to understand *how* their brain is weighing the ideas of the topic, and what their personal perspective is on it. Then, ask them if they recognize or sense any change of perspective (noting it's okay if they don't). *Learning at this level should include self-awareness of the act of learning.* That is the very definition of metacognition.

## 2. Mentee Engagement:

Engagement is critical to learning. As noted in *Connection before Content*, we must first capture their attention and then provide our mentees with a wide variety of examples, tools, and real-life experiences to cement the lesson. Hands-on and/or kinesthetic (moving, body connected) learning is even better.

Components of engagement:

- **Academic:** Your audience/mentee shows up, is attentive, asks questions, and completes tasks.

- **Intellectual:** Differentiate your teaching and mentoring; make it culturally relevant; give real-world examples; compel curiosity; create opportunities for advancement.
- **Social-emotional:** These include personal relationships, class connectivity, discussion groups, partners, mentorships.

A key idea is to tap internal motivators. Energize and inspire your mentees. Challenge them to think about a time when they have learned a topic that was energizing. How did that awaken dreams or a passion to act? Encourage that continued learning.

## 3. Storytelling

Storytelling can allow you to create compelling engagement with content. (See andragogy.) Situating your lesson in a story (fictional, real, perceived, etc.) encourages a connection which can then deepen understanding and enhance sense-making. (See transfer of knowledge.) Storytelling is the essence of the old-fashioned case study that we have all seen and used.

Storytelling in teaching has several facets. When instructors encourage story sharing *from* students, they learn about lives outside the classroom and can make more explicit connections to content, enhancing knowledge transfer. When instructors use stories to situate a theory or idea in a real-world scenario, students (particularly those with diverse learning styles) can suddenly *see* the application and better understand how and why it matters. Lastly, students gain insight into the human teacher when instructors share their own story, perhaps helping equalize the inherent power dynamic which will again enhance learning.

Read more on narrative transportation theory to see how storytelling can move an audience toward deep engagement and understanding. Dive in here. There is a lot to discover about storytelling in teaching. Storytelling is one of the most powerful engagement strategies for almost any audience. Emily Baxstrom's article, *Storytelling in the Classroom* (Nov. 1, 2016 at ohio.edu/news), outlines innovative teaching methods that anyone can try. Making real connections is key.

## 4. Bloom's Taxonomy

Bloom's hierarchical model (revised 2001) categorizes learning objectives into increasing levels of complexity. Note that the first level, remembering (information) is foundational (a necessary precondition) for putting the subsequent skills and abilities into practice.

- Remember
- Understand
- Apply
- Analyze
- Evaluate
- Create

How might you challenge your mentee to take an idea you present and apply it in their life? Afterward ask if they could they analyze and evaluate it to ultimately reach the point where they deploy it to create something new (or propel themselves to a new level).

## 5. Fink's Significant Learning

In Fink's research (2003), the components of significant learning are interactive, but not hierarchical. They may also be used selectively, depending on the context. Imagine your mentee moving through these steps:

1. Foundational Knowledge: understanding and remembering information and ideas.
2. Application: skills, critical thinking, creative thinking, practical thinking, and managing projects.
3. Integration: connecting information, ideas, perspectives, people, or realms of life.
4. Human Dimension: learning about oneself and others.
5. Caring: developing new feelings, interests, and values.
6. Learning How to Learn: becoming a better student/person, inquiring about a subject, becoming a self-directed learner.

## 6. Teacher (mentor) Immediacy:

Few people think about this. But could you take time to consider the *"nonverbal and verbal behaviors that reduce physical and/or psychological distance"* (Gorham and Christophel, 1995) between yourself and who you are mentoring? Here are some considerations:

- Where do you stand (or sit)? Are you in a position of power or equality?
- How do you speak? With humility or with authority? Can you do both?
- What is your attitude toward your mentee?
- Are *you* present? (Think about that one! Are you completely there, or worried/distracted/etc.?)

Before any encounter with a mentee, a mentor should invest time in pressing pause on all the other activities and priorities on their to-do list. They should focus on this one interaction with their mentee. Then and only then can they truly hope to have impact.

## 7. Innovative Teaching:

Here are several questions to stimulate your thinking and approach:

1. How might you give your audience notable control over the topic (course / program)? Could you adjust the mentoring schedule and your proposed learning outcomes to reflect the audience / student / mentee and *their* interests?
2. Could you present a diverse array of examples to embrace DEI (diversity, equity, inclusion)?
3. Could you identify a pressing issue that your mentee is currently experiencing and invite them to co-create a context-specific solution informed by research?
4. Could you construct a service-learning component in which your mentee might address an urgent issue facing their community or a grassroots organization? Then, solve it collectively.

## 8. Inclusive Teaching:

Inclusive teaching describes approaches to teaching or mentoring that consider the diverse needs and backgrounds of participants to create a learning environment where everyone feels valued and has equal access and opportunity to learn. Here is a popular construct for inclusion:

**VARK** (Fleming, 1987)

- **Visual** learners: partial to seeing and observing pictures, diagrams, written directions.
- **Auditory** learners: prefer listening to a lecture than reading it.
- **Reading/writing** learners: prefer writing, reading articles or books, looking up words.
- **Kinesthetic** learners: (tactile) learn through experiencing or doing things.

How are those you are mentoring wired? Are they visual, auditory, readers, or movers?

## 9. Universal Design for Learning (UDL)

This is your framework to make your coaching or mentoring flexible to meet the needs of anyone (think VARK and 8-Smarts) and reduce barriers to learning. UDL guidelines help you design your delivery to:

- Support the *why* (affective) network by providing multiple, flexible options for engagement (i.e., Why do participants care? See andragogy section.)
- Support the *how* (strategic) network by providing multiple, flexible methods of expression (i.e., What differing methods might you offer to allow mentees to demonstrate learning?
- Support the *what* (recognition) network by providing multiple, flexible methods of representation (i.e., Could you offer different content delivery choices: text, video, audio, graphs, etc.?)

## 10. Creating a welcoming, respectful learning environment:

Think about mentoring methods that consider diverse learning preferences, abilities, and *ways of knowing*. Don't forget to consider prior experience and knowledge. Learning about your mentee's personal and cultural background can improve your approach in mentoring.

Bottom line? Be open. And above all, remember to smile.

## 11. Neurodivergent Mentees:

Some of our students, audience members, and mentees may have been diagnosed with learning differences. These provide both strengths and challenges. Examples may include students with ADHD (hyper-focused, high-energy learners who may struggle with executive functioning) or students with autism (detail-oriented, high memory potential who may exhibit more anxiety or have difficulty connecting with classmates). How might you include them?

I suggest reading up on these differences to learn more. This can help you gain skills to better engage and help them in their endeavors.

## 12. Critical Pedagogy:

Paulo Freire (1968) encouraged us to help our audiences and students develop a *"critical consciousness"* so they could have the ability to recognize and analyze systems of inequality. Freire then challenged us to take action to make improvements. This will help your mentee(s) develop a sense of their own power in our social world. This approach closely relates to critical thinking. Of course, there are numerous related examples of positive change occurring (such as the Civil Rights Movement) when people took the time to pause and think critically about an issue. How might we challenge our mentees in this manner?

Freire suggests:

- Consider how you might democratize the production of knowledge (co-construction) and expand opportunities for students and faculty (or your mentee) to work and learn together as equals.
- How might you encourage students (or your mentee) to construct a positive, healthy future for themselves and their communities (pursuant to whatever your subject matter may be) that is more equable, democratic, sustainable, and just.
- How might you teach students (or your mentee) how to collaborate and take action together (again, specific subject matter notwithstanding). This can include how to engage, listen deeply, recognize power dynamics, include diverse voices, and creatively solve problems.

## For additional reading:

OSU Drake Institute for Teaching - https://drakeinstitute.osu.edu/instructor-support/inclusive-teaching

The Faculty Lounge, Harvard Business School Publishing - https://hbsp.harvard.edu/the-faculty-lounge/

## Teaching / Engagement Strategy #9

## Write Your Teaching / Mentoring Philosophy Statement

**Purpose:** *Teaching* is the work of mentoring. As mentors, we must hone our teaching skills so we can better serve our mentees. Hence, do you have a teaching, or in this case, mentoring philosophy?

**Overview:** Most mentors (most people for that matter) have not been trained as educators and have never taken even an online seminar on teaching. That's okay. This segment is designed to help you compose a *mentoring philosophy* that will help you become better. When we reflect and refocus, we gain clarity and can hold that deeper *why* in the backs of our minds while engaging in conversations. Again, this is the metacognition element that *informal* mentoring may easily miss.

**The Process:** In this section, you will reflect on your story. Specifically, I want you to articulate *why* you are becoming a mentor. Think about your core beliefs and values (things that really matter to you). An effective mentoring philosophy demonstrates that you are reflective and purposeful about reaching and teaching. It communicates mentoring goals and corresponding actions in your discussions.

Every mentor should be able to articulate their approach to and goals in mentoring. Below are some questions, ideas, and examples that may help you write or bolster your mentoring philosophy.

**Getting Started:** Fill in the blanks below. Think about these prompts. Jot down a few ideas.

**Prompt #1:**

What are your core beliefs and values? What really matters to you? Ask yourself, *"How do I, as a mentor, want to be remembered by my mentee(s)?"*

**Prompt #2:**

Now think about your own emotional intelligence (EQ). How do you recognize your own emotions? How do you recognize the emotions of others? How do you use emotional information to guide your mentoring engagement? How do you use insights and data (clues from your mentee) to guide discussions?

**Prompt #3:**

Now look for patterns or themes. Combine, organize, curate. Circle *keywords* that can become the anchors for your mentoring philosophy.

Now, begin writing. Here are some prompts:

- The purpose of mentoring is to_____.
- When mentoring my goals include _____.
- The most effective methods for mentoring are _____.
- The most important aspects of my mentoring include _____ _____.

Then write your statement using the words above that stand out to you.

- As a mentor, I will strive to _____ _____.

Section 5

# The Summary

## In summary:

Encourage someone. Those two words summarize this entire book. Encouragement is what mentoring is all about. As Kelly Kullberg wrote in her recommendation of this book, the very word encouragement derives from *"Cor,"* the Latin root of *encourage*, which means heart. Though we are prompting personal and professional development, it starts with the heart. Mentoring instills courage.

Encourage someone. This is an instruction for life. And it has a dual impact. If you are feeling down or sad or tired or depressed, *go encourage someone*. Taking action will help *you* to feel better. It will lift your spirit as it lifts theirs. This is a remarkable symbiotic truth. Like love, the more encouragement you give away, the more you receive.

Encourage someone. I am so thankful for my family, and for those teachers, pastors, mentors, friends, co-workers, and even occasional strangers who encouraged me. I am certain some of them did not know they did anything. Every smile, nod, or outright cheer helped me persist when I felt like quitting. During undergrad years, I would have dropped out were it not for my sisters encouraging me to return and, *"Just finish your degree!"*

Encourage someone. Take a moment to shine a light in someone's life. Help them to take the next step forward, even when they don't yet believe in themself. Think broadly, but start with your family. This book would not exist without that kind of help. My spouse and daughters, my brother and sisters, nieces and nephews, parents and grandparents (whether living or passed on to Heaven from earth), all are part of this manual. I am grateful beyond measure. And I am hopeful as well. *My hope is that some of the ideas you've read have both challenged and encouraged you, and that you will use some of these conversations to challenge and encourage others you mentor.*

Encourage someone. This is one of the most important things you can do in life. You could be the light that improves, or even saves, someone's life.

Thank you for reading and studying and applying some of the ideas in this book. Through your conversations, you are becoming an *Encouraging Mentor*.

# Acknowledgements

I am extraordinarily grateful for the help I've had in making this project possible. It's my mission in life to encourage as many people as I can, but I must first acknowledge the encouragement I have received. It's been remarkable.

I'm grateful to my family: Jill, my spouse of 25 years, and our daughters Abbey and Claire who have taught us more than we can imagine, and brought us more joy than we knew was possible. The love, support, and encouragement of my immediate and extended family helped write this book. I'm indebted to my editors, proofreaders, and legal reviewers: Kaitlyn Caughfield, Ruhika Roy, Clint Morrison, and so many others. I'm grateful for my colleagues and students who, over the years, have given me ideas and inspiration, all of which has energized the writing of this book.

Finally, I must thank the team at WestBow Press, and their affiliated friends at the Thomas Nelson and Zondervan publishing houses. They have been wonderful. I highly recommend them to my fellow writers.

# About the Author

Dr. Brian Raison's life mission is to encourage others. He has endeavored to practice this serving The Ohio State University for over 25 years. As a professor, he teaches on campus and statewide helping students and Ohioans build capacity so they can improve their lives and livelihoods.

His teaching and research focus on leadership (coaching, mentoring, professional development), strategic alignment (at organizational scale), and work in understanding the power of diversity for mission attainment. He's passionate about improving connections to effect positive change.

Along with his role as a Faculty Affiliate in the OSU Michael V. Drake Institute for Teaching & Learning, Brian serves as a Leadership Field Specialist with OSU Extension and teaches graduate courses in the Dept. of Agricultural Communication, Education, and Leadership. He holds a BS from OSU's Fisher College of Business, a master's in Sociology from Ohio University, Athens, and a PhD in Extension Education (non-formal andragogy and research) also from Ohio State.

Brian volunteers with his family in several faith-based service organizations across the U.S. and overseas. He carries on storytelling and heirloom gardening traditions learned from his grandparents.

# Also Available:

**40 Conversations: A Guided Journal for Personal and Professional Growth**

*Clarify your purpose. Advance your career. Create the future you want.*

Copyright © 2024 by Brian Raison, PhD

This companion journal features questions from "The Encouraging Mentor." It's a fillable workbook—a perfect resource for people you are mentoring.

This journal also works as an *independent study* for personal and professional growth. It is a great gift for those who are:

- **graduating** (to hone their purpose, resume, or grad school applications)
- **early career** (to reflect on their strengths and leverage opportunities)
- **feeling stuck** (to help redefine their work or life mission)
- **nearing retirement** (to refocus and redirect their next stage of life)

This journal also works exceptionally well for:

- small group studies
- leadership and mentoring programs

Ordering information is available here: **http://encouragingmentor.com**

# 40 Conversations:
## A Guided Journal for Personal and Professional Growth

Clarify your purpose.
Advance your career.
Create the future you want.

Name:

Brian Raison, PhD

www.ingramcontent.com/pod-product-compliance
Lightning Source LLC
Chambersburg PA
CBHW020652220526
45464CB00001B/397